UNDERSTANDING THE SACRAMENTS TODAY

Understanding the Sacraments Today

LAWRENCE E. MICK

THE LITURGICAL PRESS
Collegeville, Minnesota

Nihil obstat: Robert C. Harren, J.C.L., *Censor deputatus.*

Imprimatur: ✛ George H. Speltz, D.D., Apostolic Administrator, Diocese of St. Cloud. June 26, 1987.

Cover design by Monica Bokinskie.

Library of Congress Cataloging-in-Publication Data

Mick, Lawrence E., 1946–
    Understanding the sacraments today / Lawrence E. Mick.
        p.   cm.
    ISBN 0-8146-1567-8
    1. Sacraments—Catholic Church.   2. Catholic Church—Doctrines.
3. Catholic Church—Liturgy.   I. Title.
BX2200.M49   1987
265—dc19   87-18819
                                                                              CIP

CONTENTS

FOREWORD

The material that forms this book first appeared as a series of leaflets published by The Liturgical Press. Designed for mass distribution, the leaflets attempted to provide an explanation of the sacraments that could be easily understood by the average member of the Church. They have now been published in book form so that these explanations may be more easily used in classes or group discussions.

The liturgical renewal in the Roman Catholic Church since the Second Vatican Council (1962–65) has resulted in significant changes both in the way the sacraments are celebrated and in the way they are understood in the Church today. Adjusting to those changes has not always been easy, and often the changes in practice have occurred without an adequate appreciation of the change in understanding that gave rise to the new rituals. There is great need today for the Christian people to recover the richness of their tradition of worship. Understanding the sacraments as they are celebrated in our own time can be a crucial first step in that recovery.

A number of principles undergird the renewal of the sacraments mandated by the Second Vatican Council. Most of them are discussed in the course of the following chapters, but it might be helpful to note them briefly here at the outset. Though different principles will be discussed in connection with different sacraments, they all apply to each of the sacraments.

One of the most basic principles of the liturgical renewal is the active participation of the community of the faithful. The Constitution on the Sacred Liturgy put it this way: "Mother Church earnestly desires that all the faithful should be led to that full, conscious, and active participation in liturgical celebrations which is demanded by the very nature of the liturgy" (no. 14). That principle is not just a pastoral preference to get people more involved in religion, but it flows, as the Council noted, from "the very nature of the liturgy." Sacraments are the actions of the Church community, not simply the actions of a priest or other minister. And their effects are important to the whole community, not just to the persons who "receive" the sacraments. There are always individuals who are central to the celebration, of course. The community celebrates around those who are baptized or ordained or anointed. But it is the whole community that celebrates. The sacrament is the action of the Church, and its meaning and effects are not limited to those central individuals. That point cannot be stressed too strongly, for it may well be the most important yet least understood principle of the current renewal of our worship.

A second principle is that a sacrament is a ritual moment that is part of a larger process. Sacraments do not stand alone. They are peak moments that articulate what God is doing in our lives. They celebrate the grace of God that calls us to conversion and membership in the Church and gifts us with the Holy Spirit, that offers us reconciliation and healing, that calls some to positions of leadership in the Church community and others to the vocation of Christian marriage, and that invites us into the mystery of Christ's death and resurrection. If there is no process occurring in our lives or no awareness of the process, then there is no foundation for celebration, and the sacraments become empty rituals or magic gestures.

Ritual celebrations are composed of symbolic actions that seek to express what words cannot contain. Unfortunately we have lost much of our appreciation of symbols in our culture as well as in the Church. Many people speak in derogatory tones of "mere symbols." Yet we have always said that sacraments are "outward signs," and St. Thomas Aquinas taught that sacraments cause their effects by signifying. Symbols are a very rich form of human communication and interaction. They offer us a way to express and deal with realities that are almost inexpressible, those deep divine and human realities like love and life and death and hope and fear and joy. Without symbols we would be struck mute before the most important realities of life. Symbols enable us to grapple with the things that really matter, and a recovery of our appreciation of symbols would go a long way in helping us appreciate the richness of the sacraments.

Because of their richness, however, symbols are also ambiguous. Their meaning is clarified in the sacraments by the proclamation of the Word of God. That is another principle of the reform of the liturgy. The sacraments have always included the Word of God, of course. The very formulas and prayers of the celebrations have been drawn from the Sacred Scriptures, and God's Word is what makes the sacraments effective symbols. But the revised rites for the sacraments all include a formal proclamation of the Word of God as well. This increased attention to the Word of the Lord restores a balance between word and action that had been lost in recent centuries.

Recognizing these principles in action can help us to understand many of the changes that have occurred in the way the sacraments are celebrated. The treatment of each sacrament in this book attempts to highlight these basic principles in the course of the discussion. Different sacraments are approached in different ways, but in each case the goal is the same: to help the reader understand these central rituals of the Christian faith and come to appreciate more deeply what great gifts God has given us in the sacraments.

Sacraments of Initiation

Chapter 1

BAPTISM
Sacrament of Initial Conversion

One of the saddest episodes in the history of the Catholic Church is the Galileo case. Through his studies in astronomy, Galileo came to the conclusion that the earth revolves around the sun and that the sun is the center of the solar system.

That seems obvious to us now, but to the people and Church leaders of the time, it was a radical and dangerous idea. Everyone knew that the earth is the center of the universe, and theologians felt that the Bible confirmed that, for Christ came to earth and not to any other planet. As a result, Galileo's theory was seen as a threat to the faith, and he was ordered to change his views. He refused and was condemned, a mistake that still embarrasses the Church and makes some scientists suspicious of the Church's openness to their work.

We should not be too hard on the people of that age, however, for such a shift in perspective does not come easily. Though not as vast in scale, a similar shift is taking place within the Catholic Church in our own time. Our view of baptism is undergoing a shift from seeing infant baptism as the center of our understanding to putting adult baptism in that central position. Such shifts in perspective take time to assimilate, and the Church at large is only gradually revising its understanding of baptism and all that it entails.

This shift in perspective is really a part of a larger shift that has been occurring in recent years. We have begun to see more and more that the Christian life is an adult religion that requires an adult faith. This does not mean that there is no place for children in the Church. Jesus said, "Let the children come to me" (Matt 19:14), and the Church has always included children among its members. But as one wit put it, Jesus taught adults and played with children, while we have tended to teach children and play with adults! Increasingly we are recognizing that adult education and adult religious formation are central to the Church's life and work.

Much of the impetus for that realization has come as a result of the Second Vatican Council and its stress on the Church as the whole People of God and the importance of the laity in the Church. That same Council called for the revision of all the rites of initiation, including the restoration of the catechumenate for adults. "Restoration" is the key word, for the catechumenate is an ancient structure in the Church. The Consilium for the Implementation of the Decrees of the Council drew heavily on the ancient pattern in the formation of the Rite of Christian Initiation of Adults (RCIA), which was issued in 1972.

A Look at Our History

Before we look at the RCIA, it will be helpful to gain a sense of the history of Christian initiation through the ages. We know precious little about the rites of initiation or the preparation for them in the New Testament period. The Scriptures do indicate that baptism was conferred in the name of the Trinity (e.g., Matt 28:19) and perhaps sometimes in the name of the Lord Jesus (e.g., Acts 8:16). Romans 6 suggests that baptism may have been conferred through immersion in a pool, which was seen as going down into the tomb with Christ and rising to new life. We know from archeological evidence that this is how baptism was celebrated in the following centuries, but it is also possible that the rite developed after New Testament times in accord with Paul's symbolic description.

In any case, we do know that baptism in the early centuries of the Church's life was primarily baptism of adults. From the day of Pentecost on, the early Christians preached the gospel to adults and called them to a conversion of life that was celebrated in baptism. It is likely that children were also baptized when whole families and households were converted, but the majority of those initiated into the Church were adults.

It is also clear from various references in the writings of early Church Fathers that there were various types of preparation for initiation. In the third, fourth, and fifth centuries that preparation developed into a full-blown structure called the "catechumenate." Designed as a support and stimulus for the process of conversion, the catechumenate was a long-term experience. Persons who sought to join the Christian community were examined as to their intentions and their way of life. If those were in accord with the gospel, the inquirers were admitted into the order of catechumens. They were instructed over a period of two or three years, while sharing the Christian way of life and joining in prayer and worship with the community on Sundays. They were generally dismissed after the homily, however, since the Eucharist was only for the baptized. Their sponsors, who had brought them to the community and vouched for them, accompanied them throughout the process of their preparation and also served as their sponsors for the celebration of the sacraments of initiation.

Various liturgical rites were celebrated with the catechumens as they continued their journey toward baptism. When the candidates, their sponsors, and the community agreed that the catechumens were ready for the sacraments, their names were enrolled for baptism and they were called "the enlightened ones." The enrollment began a period of intensive spiritual preparation for the reception of the sacraments, generally lasting forty days. As the whole community began to share in that time of retreat with the initiates, it developed into the season we call Lent.

Throughout the catechumenate the progress of the candidates was celebrated with a variety of rituals and liturgies. The question that was constantly being asked was whether the Spirit of God was bringing about a true conversion in the lives of the catechumens. It was the recognition of God's action in their lives, changing them and making them new, that was the basis of the rituals that the community celebrated around them.

The culmination of the catechumenate came at the Easter Vigil, when the initiates were baptized, confirmed, and brought to the Eucharistic table for the first time. That was the night of nights, the Church's annual celebration of the death and resurrection of the Lord, manifested concretely in the new Christians who died and rose in baptism. The whole community rejoiced with them as it welcomed them into the order of the faithful. Following the reception of the sacraments, the new Christians entered a period of mystagogia, a time for reflection and meditation on the "mysteries," which was the early term for the sacraments. That was also a time for them to adjust to their new responsibilities as full members of the community, sharing fully in the life and work of the Church.

That classical form of the catechumenate was in its prime in the third, fourth, and fifth centuries. Following that period it began to decline rather rapidly, and the unified structure of initiation into the Church began to come apart. There were a variety of reasons for the decline, including the mass conversions of the German and Slavic tribes. Since they were largely nomadic tribes, they were not in one place long enough for an extended period of formation. But the most important reason was the shift toward infant baptism. Since most adults had already become Christians, the majority of baptisms being celebrated gradually became baptisms of infants. The teaching of St. Augustine and others on original sin prompted an even stronger emphasis on the baptism of infants as soon as possible after birth.

At the same time confirmation became separated from baptism, largely because it was reserved to the bishop. In the East the baptizing priest was permitted to confirm at the same ceremony, but in the West Pope Innocent I in 412 insisted that the anointing on the forehead with chrism must be done by the bishop. As dioceses grew larger, it became impossible for the bishop to be present at all the celebrations of baptism at the Easter Vigil, so the anointing was deferred until he could come. Over the centuries the gap between baptism and the anointing widened further and further, reaching as much as fourteen years in recent centuries. In the process we have come to see confirmation as a separate sacrament, an idea that would have been unthinkable to the early Church.

The Second Vatican Council called for the rite of confirmation to be revised in such a way that its intimate connection with baptism would be made clear. While the new Rite of Confirmation issued in 1971 made some strides in that direction, that connection has been made most clear in the Rite of Christian Initiation of Adults.

The Rite of Christian Initiation of Adults (RCIA)

The RCIA re-establishes the catechumenate as the structure of adult initiation in the Catholic Church. There are four major periods in the initiation process described by the rite. Those periods are separated by various liturgical rituals, which articulate and celebrate what is occurring in the process.

1. THE PRECATECHUMENATE

The first period is called the precatechumenate, which is a time of evangelization, a time for the Church to proclaim the Good News of Jesus to those who come to find out what the Church believes. On the part of the inquirers, it is a time for questioning and a time in which their intentions can mature and become clear. It involves an initial call away from sin and a first introduction to Christ and the community that follows his way of life. This period may last for several years; when it concludes it should leave the inquirers with a solid grounding in the fundamentals of the spiritual life and Christian teaching.

Rite of enrollment as catechumens

When inquirers come to the point of deciding to join the Church, they are formally enrolled in the catechumenate proper. This rite, celebrated in the midst of the Church community, includes a signing with the cross, an optional exorcism and renunciation of false worship, and an enrollment of names in the book of catechumens. By this rite the inquirers enter the order of catechumens, becoming members of the Church, though not yet baptized and thus not members of the order of the faithful. They have certain rights in the Church, including the right to Christian marriage, to Christian burial, and to special places in church. They also have the responsibility to minister to the rest of the Church, especially by sharing their conversion experience with the faithful.

At least by this point, the catechumens are to have sponsors, either chosen by them or appointed by the community. The sponsors are to walk with them and share with them throughout their journey through the catechumenate, providing a one-to-one relationship in which faith may be shared and support may be given. The rite does provide for the possibility that someone else may serve as godparents, but in practice it is usually the sponsor who fills this role as well.

2. THE CATECHUMENATE

The period of the catechumenate proper may also last for several years. It is a time of instruction in Christian doctrine, a time for association with Christians in their way of life, a time for sharing in public worship, especially celebrations of the Word, and a time for engaging in Christian service along with others in the community. In short, it is a time for experiencing the Christian way of life by involvement with the Church community in all its activities.

This period includes a variety of rites, including minor exorcisms (prayers to overcome the power of sin) and blessings, seasonal liturgies of the Word, and prayer services. The catechumens also attend the Sunday liturgy with the faithful, but they are to be dismissed after the Liturgy of the Word, since the Liturgy of the Eucharist is properly celebrated only by the baptized. This does not mean that they are to be banished to the parking lot, but that they are to be dismissed to their own gathering, where they pray and reflect together on the meaning of the Word they have heard.

The rite of election

When it is determined by the candidates, their sponsors, their catechists, and the community that the catechumens are ready for the celebration of the sacraments of initiation, they enter the period of purification and enlightenment. This period generally coincides with the season of Lent, and it begins with a rite called the "election," celebrated at Mass on the First Sunday of Lent. The election is not a ballot but a celebration of the choice (which is what "election" means) of the candidates by the Church (and thus by God) for admission to the sacraments. The rite includes the testimony of the godparents as to the readiness of the catechumens and may ask for the assent of the whole congregation. Then the names of the candidates are written in the book of the elect, and special prayers are said over them before they are dismissed.

If godparents other than the sponsors are chosen, they are to be involved in these rites and to accompany the candidates throughout the rest of the catechumenate. They also undertake an ongoing relationship with the candidates that is lifelong. The rite makes no provision for godparents who are simply honorary participants at the celebration of the sacraments; it presumes that godparents, like sponsors, will be deeply involved in the faith journey of the catechumens.

3. THE PERIOD OF PURIFICATION AND ENLIGHTENMENT

The period of purification and enlightenment is basically a time of retreat, a period of intense spiritual preparation for the reception of the sacraments. It is accompanied by several special rites, including the scrutinies, which are celebrated at Mass on the Third, Fourth, and Fifth Sundays of Lent. These rites are prayers of the whole congregation to assist the elect in strengthening what is upright and holy in their lives and overcoming what is weak and sinful. During this period there are also two presentations, at which the elect are given the Creed and the Lord's Prayer to memorize. These two texts stand as models of faith and prayer in the Christian community, and their formal presentation symbolizes the entrusting of these treasures to those who are about to join the order of the faithful.

The sacraments of initiation

At the Easter Vigil, then, the catechumenate reaches its peak with the celebration of the sacraments of initiation. The whole structure of the Vigil presumes the celebration of these sacraments as its core. After the lighting of the Easter fire and the paschal candle, the community listens to a lengthy series of readings that recount the history of God's people and also remind us of many symbols of baptism and of God's promises of salvation and new life. Following this Liturgy of the Word, the candidates renounce Satan and profess their faith. Then they are baptized (preferably by immersion), clothed in a white garment, and given a baptismal candle. Next they are confirmed by the presiding minister, whether that be a bishop or a priest. Then they take their place in the order of the faithful, leading the prayer of the faithful, presenting the bread and wine for the Eucharist, and sharing in communion for the first time.

4. THE PERIOD OF MYSTAGOGIA

Following the celebration of the sacraments, the new members of the order of the faithful are known as neophytes (newborn), and they enter the period of mystagogia. This period is described in the rite as a time for deepening the Christian experience and entering more fully into the life and unity of the faithful. With the community the neophytes meditate on the gospel, share in the Eucharist, and perform works of charity. They keep their special places in church, and their catechesis occurs primarily at Sunday Mass during the Easter period. This final phase of the catechumenate concludes with a celebration around Pentecost. The local bishop is expected to meet with the catechumens sometime within the following year, and a celebration on the first anniversary of their baptism is recommended.

This approach to adult initiation is a long way from six weeks of instructions by the pastor followed by a quiet baptism on a Saturday afternoon. The RCIA calls us to a whole new understanding and approach, not only for adult initiation but for any celebration of initiation into the Christian community.

Insights from the Adult Model

A number of insights can be drawn from the view of initiation contained in the RCIA. The first is the realization that initiation is a long-term process. For too long we have looked at sacraments simply as isolated moments, forgetting that they require both preparation and follow-up if they are to be fully effective. That is true of all the sacraments, but it may be especially true of the initiation sacraments. Coming to belong to a community of faith is something that takes time. It involves many different aspects of one's life and can be accomplished only gradually. The RCIA calls us to pay much more attention than we have in the past to the spiritual, psychological, and social dynamics of joining the Church.

The RCIA also helps us to understand the role of rituals as articulations of the process. That is especially true of the sacraments, our premier rituals, but the catechumenate includes a variety of rituals that mark the journey of the candidates. Those rituals express and celebrate what God has been doing in the lives of the initiates, and they make no sense unless there is, in fact, something happening in their lives. Neither sacraments nor other rituals are magical actions that produce results automatically. They must be supported by an underlying process, which they articulate and celebrate. The celebration does have effects, reinforcing and stimulating the process, but those effects occur to the extent that the celebration is an honest expression of the lives of the candidates.

The RCIA also makes clear that the process underlying the sacraments of initiation is one of conversion. "Conversion" is a word Catholics have long associated with joining the Catholic Church, often from another Christian denomination. But conversion is more basic than that—it is the most basic dynamic of the Christian life. In brief, conversion is the process of turning one's life over to God. It occurs as a result of personal contact with the living God and is ultimately brought about by the action of the Holy Spirit. It involves developing a personal relationship with Christ and reforming one's life according to gospel values.

None of us can make conversion happen; it is the work of the Spirit. But the catechumenate is designed to foster the conditions in which conversion might occur and to celebrate and support the process as it occurs. That cooperation with the work of the Spirit is the proper role of the Church and is, as the RCIA insists, "the business of all the baptized." This involvement of the whole community is another insight that can be gained from the rite. Welcoming and supporting new members is the responsibility of the whole community, not just the ordained ministers or the religious professionals. The rite presumes that the rituals of initiation, including the sacraments, will be celebrated by the whole community too. They are not private matters of concern only to the immediate family. Initiation is the concern of every member of the Church, which welcomes a new brother or sister into the family of God whenever initiation is celebrated.

The support of the whole community is focused especially in the role of the sponsors. The sponsors are not just honorary figures but are to be the link between the individual candidate and the larger parish community. The sponsor is to be a friend to the candidate, one who can share faith and prayer, one who introduces other members of the community, and one who models what living the Christian life means. This active and intensive role of the sponsor is another insight that can be gleaned from the catechumenate.

Finally, we might take note of the RCIA's insistence on the unity of the three sacraments of initiation. Going beyond previous documents, this rite assumes that the three sacraments of initiation will be celebrated together and empowers the priest who presides to confirm the initiates in order to make that possible. In fact, the introduction to the rite goes so far as to say that an adult is not to be baptized unless he or she receives confirmation during the same ceremony. "This connection signifies the unity of the paschal mystery, the close relationship between the mission of the Son and the pouring out of the Holy Spirit, and the joint celebration of the sacraments by which the Son and the Spirit come with the Father upon those who are baptized" (no. 34). The rite also presumes that initiation takes place within the Eucharist and calls the celebration of the Eucharist "the culminating point of their initiation" (no. 36).

Infant Baptism

Taking the adult rite as our model for understanding Christian initiation leads many to ask whether we should continue baptizing infants, and if so, under what conditions and in what circumstances. Such questions can be helpful, for they urge us to reflect anew on what our tradition of infant baptism means.

The tradition of infant baptism is apparently an ancient one. Scholars differ on just how early we can prove the practice, but it is clearly not a modern innovation. Some scholars suggest that the New Testament references to the conversion of households would have involved the baptism of children and even infants. Early examples of epitaphs on tombs of Christians also suggest initiation at a very early age. Whenever the practice began, it appears to have raised no great problem for the Church, for we find almost no record of opposition to the practice in ancient writings.

After nearly two thousand years of baptizing infants, no one should expect the Church to drop the practice today! It is a natural impulse for Christian parents to want to share their faith-life with their children throughout the time they raise them and to bring them into contact with Christ at the earliest opportunity.

Moreover, the practice of baptizing infants reminds the whole Church that salvation comes to all of us at God's initiative. God always makes the first move; only after God reaches out to us can we begin to respond. It also reminds us that God deals with us where we are and expects from us a response appropriate to our abilities at the time. Since an infant responds to its world primarily through its parents, it is logically the parents who bring the child to the community for initiation. As the parents give the child their language, their name, their style of living, their nationality, and their culture, so they also share with their children their faith and their Church identity.

Requirements for baptism

Understanding that this is what parents are doing in asking to have their child baptized can help us to understand the conditions that the Church requires before it can celebrate such a baptism. Since baptism is always a celebration of faith, there must be people of faith around whom the community can celebrate. In adult initiation the faith of the candidates themselves provides that focus; in infant baptism the faith of the parents and sponsors is central to the celebration. While the whole community has an obligation to support the faith of the initiates, in reality it is nearly impossible for the child to grow in faith without at least minimal support from one or both parents. Hence, there must be a real commitment on the part of the parents to live the gospel in their own lives. Since the community, often through the pastor, must be assured that the child will be raised in the faith, that commitment must also be manifested concretely by the parents' actions and lifestyle.

Parents are the first teachers of their child in the ways of faith, and so it is very important that they have a clear sense of the meaning of baptism and of the responsibilities they are undertaking. It is for that reason that the Rite of Baptism for Children insists that parents should be provided with suitable materials, instructions, and visits to prepare them for the baptism. Many parishes accomplish such preparation through periodic classes for parents seeking baptism for their children; other parishes may do it through home visits and printed materials. However it is done, this preparation is a valuable opportunity for the parents to deepen their faith and their understanding of the Christian way of life.

It is not enough, however, for the parents to believe in Christ or even to live by Christian principles. Baptism is fundamentally initiation into the Church, so active Church membership is also a prerequisite. Parents who never or only rarely worship with the community and who have no concrete sense of belonging or commitment to the local Church cannot honestly promise to raise their children in the Church. When that is the case, the Church cannot honestly celebrate baptism, no matter how much the pastor or the parish community would like to welcome the child into their midst. To do so would be a travesty of the sacrament, saying in ritual something that is not true in fact.

Many people have been upset in recent years by this Church policy, and many feel that it is a change in the Church's practice. In fact, this has always been the Church's policy; only when it was assured that the child would be raised in the faith could baptism be celebrated. What has changed are the conditions of modern society, in which many people have drifted away from the faith. In the past the Church could reasonably assume that any child brought for baptism would be raised in the faith. But today many people request baptism simply for cultural reasons or because the grandparents want it or out of some vague fear of condemnation if the child dies without baptism. And many of those parents have left the Church or at least dropped all active practice of their faith and membership in the Church. In the face of such circumstances, the Church more often finds it necessary to postpone baptism until there is some reasonable hope that the child will be raised in the Church.

Baptism and original sin

What upsets most people is the sense that postponing baptism is punishing the child for the parents' failures by denying him or her the chance for salvation. This conclusion rests on the assumption that unless the child is freed from original sin through baptism, he or she cannot get to heaven. That, however, is a misunderstanding of the Church's teaching on original sin. It is true that for those called to be Christians, baptism is the normal way to be freed from the power of sin. But the Church has also clearly taught that many people in the world who do not know of Christ can be saved without formal baptism as long as they respond to the gifts God has given them. Whether Buddhist, Hindu, atheist, or unbaptized child of once-Christian parents, a person is judged by God only according to what that person has been given. If the parents decide not to live a life of faith that they can share with their child, the child will not be held accountable by God for living up to a faith he or she was never given. If the child comes to faith later in life, then God will expect a response appropriate to the gifts given at that time.

Moreover, baptism does not remove original sin in some magical way. We are freed from sin in baptism because we die to sin with Christ and rise to new life. While many people still see baptism as fundamentally the removal of original sin, that is only a secondary effect of baptism. Baptism is most basically an incorporation into the death and resurrection of Christ, brought about by initiation into the community that lives out that death and resurrection every day. It is in that daily dying to sin and rising to new life that the freedom from sin which is celebrated in baptism takes root and bears fruit.

Some theologians suggest that original sin can best be understood as a web of sin into which every child is born. Just reading the daily paper or watching the evening news will remind us of how pervasive sin is in our world. If left unaided by the grace of Christ, a child will grow up under the influence of sin and become a sinful person. In this view, baptism is initiating that child into the web of the Christian community, which lives by and teaches gospel values. By involvement with this community, the child experiences the power of grace and learns to live free from the power of (original) sin. Such a perspective can help us understand why the Church insists on at least some involvement with the community of faith before baptism is celebrated.

Baptism: The beginning of a journey

As we noted earlier, sacraments are not magic moments but celebrations of a process that undergirds them. When the baptism is that of an infant, the process lies mostly in the future. The ritual celebration is only a beginning, and it will not make sense unless the process follows. It calls, therefore, for a long-term commitment, a commitment to a process of conversion that will stretch over many years. That process is never completely finished, of course. We all have parts of our lives that are not completely turned over to the Lord, and full conversion is the work of a lifetime. But there is a basic conversion that the Church requires of adult initiates; bringing those baptized as infants to that basic level of conversion is the responsibility first of the parents, and then of the sponsors and the whole community which welcomed that child. That is ultimately the purpose of Catholic schools and religious education programs, but those programs are most effective when they are based on a strong family practice of faith and an ongoing involvement in the life of the Church.

The RCIA model also reminds us that sponsors (godparents) are to play a real and vital role in the life of the initiate. Too often godparents are chosen simply because they are relatives, with parents trying not to offend either side of the family by leaving someone out. The choice should be made on very different grounds, however. A godparent should be one who will be able to share the faith with the child, who will be involved in the life of the child in some real way, and who will help that child by word and example to understand what it means to live as a member of the Church. That is why the Church requires that a godparent be Catholic, be old enough to undertake the responsibility (usually at least sixteen), and be confirmed and living an active faith life. A non-Catholic may stand as one of the witnesses at the baptism, but such a witness is not a godparent, strictly speaking. Such a witness should also be actively living the Christian faith in his or her own denomination.

The perspective of the RCIA also helps us to see the importance of baptism to the whole Church community. It is for this reason that baptism should normally be celebrated in the midst of the assembly, either at Sunday Mass or in a special celebration of baptism that involves members of the Church community as well as members of the family. For too long we have looked at baptism as simply a family affair. It is always of concern to the whole Christian community.

It is important for the community to celebrate baptism regularly, for the way we initiate new members reminds us of what it means to be a member. The celebration of initiation is the chief way the community renews its own commitment to living as baptized Christians. Those who are baptized are committed to a way of life that often runs counter to the culture in which we live today. We need to be reminded often of who we are and what we are called to be. Many commentators have noted the importance of developing a deeper consciousness of our baptism in the members of the Church today. The more we realize that we are called to a different and special way of life, the better we will be able to live out the demands of the gospel. In a very deep sense, realizing the implications of our baptism is the key to our personal holiness and to the health and vitality of the Church itself. Perhaps the new rites of Christian initiation, both for adults and for infants, will help us come to that realization. Let us pray that it may be so!

DISCUSSION/REFLECTION QUESTIONS

1. Have you noticed the shift to a more adult emphasis in the Church's life since the Second Vatican Council? Where have you seen it? How has it affected your life?

2. Does your experience of Lent reflect its origins as a time of preparation for baptism? How could Lent become more of a time of baptismal renewal in your life?

3. How has the Church's approach to original sin changed in recent years? How does that affect our understanding of baptism?

4. Are you familiar with the restored catechumenate (RCIA)? If it has been restored in your parish, what is your part in it? If it has not been restored yet, how can you help the parish begin?

5. What does it mean concretely to say that initiation is "the business of all the baptized," as the RCIA states?

6. Do you participate each year in the Easter Vigil? Is it clear in your parish that this is the most important liturgical celebration of the whole year? How could that be made more obvious?

7. Is it a new idea for you that sacraments always involve a process over time? How might that affect your preparation for, and celebration of, the sacraments?

8. What does the word "conversion" mean to you? In what ways has God called you to conversion in the course of your life?

9. If the adult rites of initiation are the model for understanding baptism, how do you explain infant baptism today? Can you explain why a priest may sometimes have to postpone the baptism of an infant?

10. Why should baptism always be celebrated in the midst of the community of faith? Do you understand why the Church insists that baptisms should be celebrated where the Church usually gathers rather than in a family home?

Chapter 2

CONFIRMATION
Celebrating the Spirit of God

An old story tells of four blind men who were asked to describe an elephant. Relying on the sense of touch, one man examined a leg of the beast and said, ''An elephant is like the trunk of a tree, only not as rough.'' Another man felt the elephant's trunk and insisted, ''This animal is like a very large snake.'' The third man encountered the side of the beast and claimed, ''An elephant is obviously like a large wall,'' while the fourth examined the animal's ear and said, ''This beast is clearly like a huge leaf waving in the breeze.''

Something very similar must be happening in our time with the sacrament of confirmation. Picking up different books and listening to different speakers describe this sacrament makes one wonder if they are all talking about the same sacrament. The underlying assumption of this chapter is that many of those who write and speak on this sacrament have the same problem as the blind men: they have grasped one dimension of the sacrament and concluded that this one aspect comprises the whole reality.

Some people see confirmation as the sacrament of Christian maturity; others see it as simply the completion of baptism. Some stress the Christian commitment the sacrament requires; others emphasize the free gift of the Holy Spirit. Some argue that it must be celebrated only in late teen or early adult years; others contend that it is best celebrated with baptism, even in infancy. For some people it is the beginning of a lifetime of Christian living; for others it is the final capstone of parish religious education. Some say it makes Christians into soldiers of Christ; others, into missionaries of the gospel; still others, into servants of the world. And different writers combine several of these ideas, giving them varying degrees of importance.

Is anyone surprised that many people are uncertain about the meaning of this sacrament? Confusion seems to reign supreme. Even official documents from Rome seem almost contradictory in the way they speak about confirmation. How is the non-expert to make sense out of all of this?

This chapter will not attempt to settle all the disputes raging among religious educators, liturgists, and pastors. (Given the intensity with which some argue their position, even God might have trouble getting that kind of consensus today!) It will not even attempt to express the meaning of confirmation in any definitive way. This treatment is intended simply to help the non-expert make some sense out of the confusion, to get a broad enough view of the sacrament to begin to integrate the many different dimensions of it. Perhaps taking the broader view will help us to move closer to an eventual consensus at some point in the future.

A Look at History

One of the first steps in putting confirmation in perspective is to take a look at the history of the sacrament. Evidence from the early days of the Church is very limited. Scripture scholars tell us that despite various hints about the role of the Holy Spirit in the lives of Christians, the New Testament gives us no real evidence for any rite that we would recognize as confirmation. For several centuries after the New Testament period, Christians would have been very puzzled if asked about the sacrament of confirmation. What we have come to know as a separate sacrament was for them simply a part of the rite of baptism, the celebration of initiation by which a person became a Christian.

The celebration of initiation varied from place to place and from time to time, so it would take a large book to describe it in detail in all its variations during those centuries. Instead, we will examine here a typical outline of elements that can give us a sense of the experience. Such a rite, normally celebrated at the Easter Vigil, would begin with the candidates for initiation leaving the assembly of the faithful to go to the baptistry, often a separate building near the entrance to the church. Once there, they would renounce Satan, perhaps facing west and spitting at him; then, facing east, they would commit themselves to Christ. After that, they would strip completely, leaving their old life (and old clothes) behind. They would be anointed over their whole bodies, preparing for the crucial contest with the power of evil, like athletes being rubbed down before a match.

After the blessing of the font, the candidates would enter the water, perhaps going down three steps into a pool, where they were immersed three times in the name of the Father and of the Son and of the Holy Spirit. Coming out of the water, they would be clothed in white garments. At that point they would return to the full assembly, where the bishop was waiting with the faithful. Greeted with acclamations, they would then be anointed with chrism by the bishop and greeted with the kiss of peace. Now members of the faithful, they would join the full assembly for the celebration of the Easter Eucharist.

That final anointing by the bishop is what we have come to call confirmation. As this description of initiation suggests, the anointing was a brief part of a much larger rite. It was unique, however, in that it was done by the bishop, while the earlier parts of the rite were the responsibility of the presbyter (priest) or deacon (or deaconess). It was this uniqueness that led to its becoming a separate sacrament in the West. As long as dioceses were small and the bishop always presided at Easter initiations, there was no problem. But when that was no longer possible due to the increasing size of the Church, the question arose about what to do with that part of initiation when the bishop was not present.

In the East the decision was made that whoever presided at the Easter rites would do the anointing. In the West, however, Pope Innocent I insisted in 412 that this anointing was reserved to the bishop. Thus it became separated from the baptismal ritual. At first it was still celebrated shortly after the Easter Vigil, during Easter week or at least in the Easter season, but gradually it began to be pushed back further and further. Through the centuries the normal age for this completion of initiation was extended more and more, until finally confirmation was generally celebrated at age fourteen. As that happened, first communion was also delayed, since it was properly received only after confirmation. At the beginning of this century, Pope Pius X lowered the age for first communion to the age of discretion, generally assumed to be about age seven, to encourage more frequent communion, and confirmation was left hanging, as it were, in midair, now fully removed from the initiation celebration in most people's minds.

A Sacrament of Initiation

The liturgical renewal endorsed by the Second Vatican Council in 1963 called for a recovery of that initiation connection. The Constitution on the Sacred Liturgy issued by the Council said that the ''rite of confirmation is to be revised and the intimate connection which this sacrament has with the whole of Christian initiation is to be more clearly set forth" (no. 71). The revised Rite of Confirmation issued in 1971 reflects that concern in several ways. The candidates for confirmation renew their baptismal vows during the celebration. They are encouraged to have their baptismal godparents as sponsors for this sacrament as well, and they are also encouraged to use their baptismal names as confirmation names (though another sponsor or name may be chosen). The sacrament is now regularly celebrated within the Eucharist, thus reminding us of the ancient practice of celebrating baptism, confirmation, and Eucharist as one initiatory rite.

The Rite of Christian Initiation of Adults (RCIA), issued in 1972, goes even further in manifesting the connnection between all three sacraments of initiation. That rite, gradually being implemented in parishes across the country and around the world, has already done much to deepen our understanding of Christian initiation, and thus of confirmation. The introduction to the rite insists that "according to the ancient practice maintained in the Roman liturgy, an adult is not to be baptized unless he or she receives confirmation immediately afterward, provided no serious obstacles exist. This connection signifies the unity of the paschal mystery, the close relationship between the mission of the Son and the pouring out of the Holy Spirit, and the joint celebration of the sacraments by which the Son and the Spirit come with the Father upon those who are baptized" (no. 34). To make that possible, the rite authorizes whoever presides at the initiation of adults to confirm them, whether that be a bishop or a priest.

Thus for adults the ancient pattern has been restored. For children baptized in infancy, however, the situation is still a bit jumbled. Confirmation is regularly received after first communion, with the age ranging from seven or eight (soon after first Eucharist) to eighteen or twenty-one, depending on local policies in various dioceses and parishes.

Nevertheless, the new rite of confirmation and the RCIA give us a clear framework within which to understand this sacrament. Confirmation is a sacrament of initiation. Whenever it is celebrated and in whatever order the sacraments of initiation are received, confirmation is part of the initiation process.

A Process of Conversion

As the RCIA reminds us, initiation is intimately connected with the process of conversion. Conversion is the fundamental dynamic of the Christian way of life. We all are called to a life of continual conversion, gradually rooting out sin and selfishness and giving our lives more and more completely to Christ. Nevertheless, one's initial conversion is the basis for the celebration of the initiation sacraments. Those sacraments celebrate the conversion that God is bringing about in the lives of the candidates. When they are celebrated with adults in the RCIA, they celebrate a conversion that has already reached a certain maturity through the catechumenate formation process. When initiation begins in infancy, the sacramental celebration anticipates the conversion and presumes that the conversion will be fostered in the months and years ahead. If there is no reasonable assurance that this will happen, then the celebration of initiation must be delayed until it can be assured.

Understanding Sacraments

Though they probably never realized it, many Christians have for too long held a rather magical notion of sacraments. If the sacrament was received, it would automatically produce its result. That is true, of course, on God's side. If a person is validly baptized, God adopts that person as a son or daughter. If the Eucharist is validly celebrated, Christ is truly present in his body and blood. But the effect on us is another question. God is present and acting, but whether we benefit from the sacrament depends on our attitude and our openness, which in turn are affected by the way the sacrament is celebrated and the way we prepare for it. Thus baptism celebrated with no conversion (before or after) is of no spiritual value to the one baptized; it becomes an empty ritual, at least as far as the one baptized is concerned.

That raises another issue about our understanding of sacraments. We have generally focused, almost exclusively, on the individual(s) who "received" the sacraments. It is obvious that those people are central to the celebration, yet every sacrament is fundamentally a celebration of the Church. It is the whole assembly that celebrates the sacrament around the candidates. Sacraments are the way the Church celebrates what God is doing in the lives of its members. For an honest and fruitful celebration, there must be something happening before the Church has reason to celebrate.

What is happening is proportionate to the age and capability of the candidates, of course. If initiation is celebrated around infants, the community celebrates the fact that the children are being brought into its midst with a commitment by the parents and by the community to foster conversion to the faith that the community shares. The Church celebrates the choice of a child by God and by the family and community which promise to support that child in faith. The ancient tradition of infant initiation is a constant reminder to the Church that God always takes the initiative in our salvation. Even before the infants can respond to God's initiative on their own, God chooses them and gifts them with divine grace. It is certainly valid for the Church to celebrate that fact, as long as there is assurance that the child will be raised in the community of faith and thus come to a personal faith that corresponds to his or her growth.

When any of the sacraments of initiation is celebrated

around an older individual, the Church also celebrates the personal faith and commitment of the candidate. The community must be able to see that conversion is happening in the life of the candidate if it is to celebrate honestly. An infant responds to God, as it responds to everything, primarily through its parents; older children and adults must respond in a manner appropriate to their capability.

If there is no commitment to conversion on the part of the parents of an infant or if there is no evidence of conversion in an older candidate, then the Church must postpone the celebration. Those who must make such a decision do so reluctantly and sadly, but there really is no alternative. To celebrate what does not exist makes the sacrament into a false symbol, a time of "let's pretend and hope God takes care of it somehow." Ultimately such a sacramental celebration is a lie and a misuse of the sacrament. A true respect for the sacraments as gifts of God requires us to celebrate them honestly or not at all.

Attention to the readiness of the candidate is important for a true celebration, yet more is needed. If the sacraments are celebrations of the whole Church, the whole Church must be involved with the candidates in their conversion process. As the RCIA has helped us to understand, the initiation of new members into the Church "is the business of all the baptized" (no. 41). All the faithful are expected to take responsibility for those being initiated. They support them by prayer and fasting, they join with them in prayer and study, they make them feel welcome and give them, by example, insight into the way of life of the Christian community. That same concern should surround those who are baptized as infants and those who are confirmed and brought to first Eucharist as children. The community should manifest its interest and support as the candidates go through their gradual conversion, learning and growing in the life of Christ.

At the same time, the community itself benefits from such interaction as well. Every time initiation is celebrated around an individual or a group of individuals, the whole community is once again drawn into the conversion process. The witness of those being initiated is a powerful example to the rest of the Church. The candidates are living reminders of the community's own initiation and the commitment that it entails. While the community supports the initiates, it is also challenged by them to live up to its own identity as a people always in the process of deepening its own level of conversion. It may well be that a lack of the regular experience of the initiation sacraments by most Catholics is a major cause of the spiritual apathy in so many parishes. Those celebrations can serve as a potent reminder of who we are as a people and of what life in Christ really means.

The Meaning of Confirmation

If the sacraments of initiation, taken together, celebrate conversion, the question of the unique meaning of confirmation remains. Ever since the sacraments got separated in time in the West, the Church has struggled to find a satisfactory explanation of what confirmation does that baptism hasn't already done.

Confirmation has always been the focus of the gift of the Holy Spirit, seen often as the continuation of the Pentecost event. Yet the Church has also always associated the gift of the Spirit with baptism. Anyone who has taught about this sacrament knows the questions that raises: Do we get another ''dose'' of the Spirit? Wasn't the Spirit's coming at baptism effective? Why do we need confirmation at all? As long as the anointing was part of the same ceremony with baptism, there was no problem. In that framework the anointing and laying on of hands were the focus for the community's celebration of the gift of the Spirit, while the water bath was the focus of incorporation into the death and resurrection of Christ. Once they were separated, however, the problems were inevitable. The same issue arises with other aspects of the meaning of confirmation. Is it the sacrament of Christian witness? Yes, because the Spirit is the power within us that enables us to witness. But doesn't baptism already commit us and empower us to witness? Does confirmation make us soldiers of Christ, able to suffer for him if necessary? Yes, the Spirit gives courage to profess our faith even under persecution. But isn't that also true of baptism?

One approach that has been popular for centuries is to see baptism as the sacrament of Christian infancy, and confirmation as the sacrament of Christian maturity. The main difficulty with that approach is the definition of "Christian maturity." Many people incorrectly identify Christian maturity with either the beginning or the end of puberty. In accord with that principle, many parishes have pushed the age of confirmation back further and further in quest of some magic age when the candidates will be "mature." Christian maturity refers rather to maturity in faith. But maturity is a relative term. A ten-year-old is acting maturely when he or she acts like a ten-year-old. The Church's tradition of celebrating initiation in its fullness with both adults and children points out the inadequacy of this approach. If baptism can be celebrated with infants, so can confirmation. It is the completion of baptism, but it is not the sacrament of Christian adolescence.

What, then, is confirmation? What does it celebrate? What does it add to baptism? Well, history reminds us that when baptism and confirmation were celebrated together, the water rite focused on incorporation into the paschal mystery, the death and resurrection of Christ, while the anointing focused the community's celebration on the gift of the Holy Spirit. If we remember that sacraments are always the community's celebrations of what God is doing, then confirmation is different from baptism in that it focuses more exclusively on the Spirit who dwells among us and within us. It provides an opportunity for the Church community to celebrate the gifts and presence of the Spirit as these are manifested in the lives of the initiates. It is a time for all the members of the Church to rejoice in the Spirit they share and in the gifts the Spirit pours out on individuals for the good of all.

The question of what the community is celebrating is a different issue than what happens to the individual recipients, but the celebration also has an effect. Whenever the community celebrates a dimension of its life and conversion, that dimension is strengthened and deepened. In confirmation the whole community should become more aware of the Spirit, more open to divine guidance, more aware of the gifts they have received. Those around whom the community celebrates would naturally experience those effects even more deeply than the rest of the community, though, of course, that is not automatic. Like all spiritual effects of the sacraments, they depend on the preparation for and openness to the action of God. That is true for all who celebrate the sacrament, both the recipients and the rest of the community. The way those effects are experienced will also vary, depending on the age of the recipients. God takes each of us at our own stage of growth and gives gifts appropriate to our age and needs. But the Church is always celebrating the gifts and presence of the Spirit in its midst.

Options for the Future

God's willingness to accept us with our limits and at our own stage of growth suggests various options for the celebration of confirmation. All three sacraments of initiation (baptism, confirmation, Eucharist) can be celebrated in one ceremony in the ancient pattern. That is the official pattern for adults who join the Church through the catechumenate. Some have suggested that we ought to celebrate all three sacraments with infants too, as was done in the early Church and is still done in the tradition of the East. Others have suggested that Christian parents might wish to enroll their newborn children as catechumens and then celebrate all three sacraments of initiation at a later age. Though these two options are not possible within current Church law, the future may see more openness to such adaptations.

It may also be that the three sacraments of initiation will often be separated in time, celebrated at different stages in a Christian's growth. If so, it may be that we will return to the traditional order: baptism, confirmation, Eucharist. For the immediate future, however, the twentieth-century pattern of baptism, Eucharist, and then confirmation will obviously be common.

Which of these patterns will prevail in the future is hard to say. However the future unfolds, though, we can recognize at this point several constant factors, insights that remain true no matter at what age confirmation is celebrated or in what order the sacraments of initiation are received.

Baptismal Connection

The first factor is the intimate connection between baptism and confirmation. As we noted earlier, ever since the sacraments were separated historically and that intimate connection was forgotten, the Church has struggled to find some way to explain what confirmation is all about. The Second Vatican Council wisely recognized that the only way to really understand confirmation is to re-establish clearly its connection with baptism. At whatever age the sacrament is celebrated, and whether it is celebrated in the same ceremony as the other initiation sacraments or separated over time, that connection must never again be forgotten. Confirmation is the other side of the coin of baptism and cannot be understood apart from it.

Those who are preparing to be confirmed should reflect deeply and prayerfully on the meaning of their baptism and all its implications. Everything that baptism means and everything to which it commits us is what confirmation reaffirms. As a sacrament of initiation, confirmation is a beginning, not an ending. Too often seen as the end of a student's religious education, it should rather be the beginning of a deeper level of Christian living. As a reaffirmation of baptism, it can be a time to undertake the Christian way of life with new vigor and deeper commitment.

Fostering Conversion

A deeper commitment is the result of a deeper conversion. The process of conversion is a lifelong task, and it occurs in a multitude of ways in the life of each Christian. The preparation for and celebration of confirmation should contribute to that ongoing process. We are continually called by the Spirit to give ourselves more completely to God, to live more completely in the Kingdom. No matter how young or old we are, our conversion is still incomplete. The work of the Spirit is especially the work of conversion, for the Spirit dwells within us, nearer to us than we are to ourselves, and seeks always to draw us further into the divine life of the Trinity.

Conversion is a multifaceted reality, for it involves a personal relationship with the Lord, a change of life based on gospel principles, a relationship to all those who form the Body of Christ, and a commitment of self-sacrificing love and service to others in the name of Christ. Initiation into the Christian community involves all those dimensions, for it is incorporation into a community united by the same Lord, living the gospel way of life and seeking to love all people as God loves them. Confirmation, as a powerful experience of the Spirit, should lead to a fuller and deeper incorporation into that community and its life.

Perhaps this is a good place to remember that no sacrament is an isolated moment, separate from the experience of the Lord throughout our lives. Sacraments are like peaks we climb on our journey through life. From the peak we can see both where we have been and where we are headed. Sacraments help us to crystallize and focus what God is doing in our lives, and thus they further a process that both precedes and follows them. The reality that the sacrament celebrates is always much larger than the ritual moment.

So with confirmation, the process of conversion precedes and follows the ritual celebration. The actual timing of the ritual moment is not nearly as important as the process it celebrates. As Aidan Kavanagh insists, the real issue is not at what age to celebrate confirmation but rather what conversion is and how we foster it. Whether confirmation is celebrated around an eight-day-old or an eighty-year-old person, the Church must make sure that there is a process of conversion linked to it and flowing from it. Without such conversion the sacrament will become an empty ritual at any age.

Fostering conversion, however, is not as easy as talking about it. Conversion is truly God's work; all we can do is to try to provide an environment in which it might happen. That is less a matter of intellectual study (though that can help at times) than it is a matter of prayer and witness. Opportunities for prayer and retreat and the support of a prayerful community of faith should be part of any process of preparation for confirmation. And the personal example and testimony of those who are sincerely trying to live in the Spirit also seem essential.

Much of that witness is properly the role of the sponsor. For too long we have looked at the role of sponsor as primarily an honor bestowed on whichever aunt or uncle hasn't been one yet! Instead, as the RCIA teaches us, the role of sponsors is a vital one in the initiation process. The sponsors serve as the candidates' partners in the whole experience, supporting them by their presence and their prayer, sharing their own faith, and calling the candidates to a deeper commitment by their own example. Experience with catechumens suggests that sponsors are often the single most important dimension of the initiation experience. Sponsors should be chosen for their ability to fulfill the role rather than simply by family kinship. The sponsors might best be chosen from the local parish, since part of their role is to help the candidates become more deeply involved in the life of the Church.

Celebrating the Spirit in the Church

Confirmation is always a celebration of the Spirit in the Church. It is important that we begin to understand that it is a celebration for the whole community. Too often the preparation for and celebration of this sacrament is restricted to the candidates and their families. While the physical limitations of the church building may make it impossible for the whole parish to attend the ceremony, the parish still needs to be involved throughout the whole process. Candidates should be visible and involved in the life of the parish in a variety of ways. They should be the focus of the prayers of the parish in Sunday worship as they prepare to be confirmed. Different groups in the parish, including shut-ins, might adopt various candidates as the special focus of their prayer and witness. The celebration of confirmation in a parish ought to be an occasion for every member of the parish to reflect on and rejoice in the gifts of the Spirit he or she has received.

The community needs such "Spirit consciousness-raising" now and then if it is to truly live in that Spirit. Thus we remember who we really are: a community called to live by the Spirit of God, who constantly calls us to conversion. The Spirit is the source of our life and the binding force that unites us in divine love. May that same Holy Spirit inspire all of us to live ever more fully the way of the Lord.

DISCUSSION/REFLECTION QUESTIONS

1. What has been your main image of confirmation in the past? Has this chapter helped you to broaden your understanding of this sacrament?

2. Why do you think Pope Innocent I insisted that the final anointing during baptism be reserved to the bishop? Do you think it was a good decision, or should we have allowed the priest to complete the initiation, as was done in the East and as the RCIA does today for adult initiation?

3. What does it mean to say that confirmation is a sacrament of initiation? How does that perspective affect the way we understand confirmation? Does it have implications for the age of the candidates and/or for how we celebrate the sacrament?

4. How are conversion and the work of the Holy Spirit connected? How is that connection apparent in the way your parish prepares for confirmation? What can be done to more effectively foster conversion among the candidates for this sacrament?

5. If confirmation were celebrated with infants at the same time as baptism, when would conversion take place, and how can it be fostered by the parish?

6. Has your understanding of sacraments ever been a bit magical or automatic? How important do you think good preparation and good use of the rituals are?

7. How can we deepen our awareness of all the sacraments as community celebrations? What are the factors that keep us limited to an individualistic perspective?

8. Why is it important for the community to celebrate regularly the initiation of new members?

9. What distinguishes confirmation from baptism? How would you explain to students what is unique about confirmation?

10. What do you think will happen with the sacrament of confirmation in the future? Why?

Chapter 3

EUCHARIST
Center of the Christian Life

The Eucharist is the central sacrament of the Church. It is central both in its importance and in the frequency of its celebration. Because most Catholics celebrate it every week (and some every day), it is the most familiar of our sacramental rituals. That familiarity, however, can mask a need for greater understanding of the various elements that make up this rather complex ritual celebration.

Those of us who have grown up with the tradition of weekly Eucharist may assume that it is all very clear and straightforward. But as many non-Christian visitors have discovered, the Mass is a fairly complex ritual, and its meaning is not always self-evident. Various parts of the Mass—most of them, in fact—are very ancient, deriving from a time and a culture quite different from our own. A review of the history and meaning of those parts can help us to understand and appreciate the richness of this worship service, ever ancient and ever new.

To provide such a review is the goal of this chapter. We will examine each part of the Mass, from beginning to end, explaining its shape, its origin, and its purpose within the whole Eucharistic liturgy. There is much more that can be said about the Eucharist; volumes have been written about this sacrament without exhausting the possibilities. But re-examining what we do each time we celebrate the Eucharist can help us to see afresh the meaning of this sacrament. Sometimes the perspective of a stranger can help us to see what our familiar routine has caused us to overlook or forget.

First, though, it may be helpful to comment on some words we have already used whose meaning may not be self-evident. One is the word "liturgy." The word comes from the Greek, meaning "work of the people," and it refers to the public worship of the Church in its various forms: the Mass, the other sacraments, and the Liturgy of the Hours (psalms and prayers at various hours of the day). The focus of this chapter will be the Eucharistic liturgy, or the Mass. "Eucharist" is also from the Greek and means "thanksgiving." The Eucharist is primarily a worship service of thanksgiving. It is also called the "Mass," a term that comes from the dismissal rite of the service, meaning "the sending forth," a reminder that Christians who gather for the Eucharist are sent out again to live out its meaning in their daily lives. Throughout this chapter the terms "Mass" and "Eucharistic liturgy" are used interchangeably.

Part I: The Gathering

Although the Mass contains many traditional elements and terms, it shares the basic structure of any human celebration. Every celebration has four basic elements: gathering, listening, sharing, and sending forth. People gather and form a community to celebrate. They listen to one another or to a speaker to understand the meaning of the event. They share food, drink, conversation, and themselves in a variety of ways. Finally, they are dismissed and disperse, ending the event. These elements will be expressed formally or informally, but they will always be there in some form.

The Mass can be divided into two major parts, one including the gathering and the listening, and the other composed of the sharing and the dismissal. The first part includes the entrance rites and the Liturgy of the Word (sometimes together called the Liturgy of the Word), and the second part includes the Eucharistic rite and the dismissal (sometimes together called the Liturgy of the Eucharist or the Liturgy of the Table).

The Mass, then, begins with the gathering of Christians, the assembling of the People of God in this time and place. When all have arrived, the gathering is celebrated ritually with the entrance rites. According to the General Instruction of the Roman Missal, "the purpose of these rites is that the faithful coming together take on the form of a community and prepare themselves to listen to God's word and celebrate the Eucharist properly" (no. 24). Actually, that may be a bit much to ask from such simple rites! It is not likely that they will make people into a community if they are not one before they arrive, nor will they prepare people to hear God's Word unless they already want to hear it. What these rites can do is to make people more aware of the fact that they are a community and then help them settle down and focus their attention on the Word proclaimed in the readings. The entrance rites include the entrance song, the sign of the cross, the greeting, the penitential rite, the *Glory to God,* and the opening prayer.

The Mass begins with an entrance song, which is intended to serve several functions. Singing helps people to get into the mood of celebration and also to sense their unity, since all sing the same words at the same time and on (roughly) the same note. The entrance song is often chosen to suggest the theme of the Sunday or feast being celebrated. Originally developed to accompany the procession of the ministers to the altar, it still serves that function, even if the procession is often a short one in many churches today.

When the presiding minister (priest or bishop) reaches the altar, he reverences the altar with a kiss. The altar has been viewed for centuries as a symbol of Christ, who is the altar, the priest, and the victim of the Eucharistic sacrifice. The altar is kissed as a sign of reverence for Christ and as a sign of recognition of Christ's presence in the midst of the assembly.

After the song is completed, the presider and the people begin with the sign of the cross, invoking the Father, the Son, and the Holy Spirit and signing themselves with the symbol of Christ's victory over death. This simple gesture is a reminder to Christians of who they are and what their life means, a sharing in the death and resurrection of Christ. The presider then greets the assembly with one of three greetings, which are among the most ancient texts of the liturgy. "The Lord be with you" is found in the Old Testament in Ruth 2:4; Judges 6:12, etc. "The grace of our Lord Jesus Christ and the love of God and the fellowship of the Holy Spirit be with you all" comes from 2 Corinthians 13:13. The third greeting is also from St. Paul, who used it to open many of his letters, as in Galatians 1:3: "The grace and peace of God our Father and the Lord Jesus Christ be with you." Much more meaningful than a simple "Hello" or "Good morning," these greetings are a prayerful wish exchanged between the presider and the congregation. They are also a good example of how the texts of our liturgy are often derived from the Word of God in the Bible.

After the greeting the assembly enters into a penitential rite in most Masses. This rite is commonly misunderstood. Many people think it is designed to make us pure so that we can worthily celebrate the Eucharist. Others view it as a modern substitute for the sacrament of penance, a time to summon up feelings of guilt and repentance and to be forgiven. Actually it is a simple rite to remind us of God's great mercy and of the fact that we are already forgiven. Therefore it should deepen our joy as we gather to worship, for the focus is not on our sins but on God's mercy and faithful love. The penitential rite reminds us of another reason we have to give thanks, since we are all sinners who gather through the gracious gift of God's forgiveness. Sometimes the blessing and sprinkling with water replaces the penitential rite. This ritual gesture leads to the same sense of gratitude, but it focuses explicitly on our baptism as the first celebration of God's love and forgiveness. In any Mass that has a special opening (wedding, Palm Sunday, etc.), the penitential rite is omitted.

On Sundays (except in Advent and Lent) and major feasts, the *Glory to God* follows the penitential rite. This song of praise comes from Greek and Syrian sources in the very early centuries of the Church. It is modeled on the psalms and canticles of the Bible and contains much biblical material. Though it reminds us of the angels' Christmas greetings to the shepherds, it was originally an Easter hymn of dawn. It then found a place at the end of morning prayer in the East, and by the sixth century it found its way into the Roman Mass. Originally sung by the whole assembly, it later became a choir piece with very elaborate melodies. The recent renewal of the liturgy has returned this ancient hymn to the whole assembly as its song of praise.

The oldest and most important part of the entrance rites is the opening prayer. In the earliest centuries the Mass began with just a period of silent prayer before the reading of the Word of God. Then a short collect prayer was added for the presiding minister to "collect" the prayers of the assembly in verbal form. (That is how we still begin on Good Friday.) All the rest of the entrance rites were added later. The function of this prayer is the same as it was in the beginning: to sum up the silent prayers of the assembly. That is why it is usually rather general in its wording. That is also why there is a silent space between the invitation "Let us pray" and the collect itself. This silent time is intended to give all who are at Mass a chance to express to the Lord their personal prayers for the day.

The opening prayer brings us to the end of the entrance rites. If they have succeeded in their purpose, we are now conscious of our identity as the Body of Christ and ready to hear the Word of God. Many authors have suggested that the entrance rites today are too long and too cluttered. The addition of so many different elements over the centuries has produced a fairly lengthy beginning, and it is possible that it will be simplified in the years ahead. Whether long or short, however, these rites will only be as effective as we allow them to be. Our willingness to enter into the spirit of the day's liturgy is the most important element in the success or failure of these rites.

Part II: The Listening

The Liturgy of the Word is probably the most straightforward of the sections of the Mass. It consists of three readings (two on weekdays), responses between the readings, and the homily. Even a complete stranger would recognize this as a time of proclamation and listening.

The Word of God is proclaimed in three readings taken from a Lectionary (list of readings) that is arranged in a three-year cycle and covers most of the Bible. In the design of the cycle, the gospel was chosen first, with readings chosen from Matthew one year, Mark the next year, and Luke the third year. The Gospel of John is read during Lent and the Easter season each year; it is also used for several weeks in the summer of Mark's year. The first reading, either from the Old Testament or the Acts of the Apostles (during Easter), was chosen to relate to the gospel. The second reading, from Paul or one of the other epistles, is usually independent of the other readings, gradually moving through a given epistle week by week. On major feasts, however, all three readings follow the theme of the day.

After the first reading the congregation responds with a psalm, usually sung in responsorial form, that is, the congregation sings a repeated response, while a cantor or choir sings the verses of the psalm. Thus we respond to the Word of God by using the Word of God. Since the psalms cover a wide range of human emotions and situations, it is easy for the psalm to be chosen to respond to the first reading. It does this by echoing the theme of the reading, or by continuing a quote in the reading, or by providing an answer to the reading (for example, a psalm of hope after a reading from the Book of Job).

Before the reading of the gospel, the congregation stands and sings a gospel acclamation to honor Christ, who is present through the proclamation of the gospel. The cantor or choir sings "Alleluia" (or a substitute in Lent), the people repeat the acclamation, the cantor sings a short verse that indicates the theme of the gospel for the day, and the "Alleluia" is repeated. During the acclamation the priest or deacon who will proclaim the gospel bows before the altar in prayer and then moves to the lectern for the proclamation.

After the readings have been proclaimed, the priest or deacon seeks to break open the Word we have heard through a homily. "Homily" refers to a form of preaching that is based on the Word, not just on a topic the preacher would like to expound. The homily continues the process by which God speaks to us, applying the ancient scriptural Word to the situations of our own time and place. That Word speaks to us both as individuals and as a community; the preacher's task is to help us understand both dimensions of God's Word.

That task is not the preacher's alone, however. Each of us must be part of the process, opening our hearts and minds to the Word of the Lord. After each of the first two readings and again after the homily, there is a brief pause for silence. A visitor may think that somebody lost the place or missed a cue, but it is really a deliberate break to give us a chance to reflect on what we have heard and ask ourselves how it applies to us. The Word of God always demands a change if we truly hear it; we need time to reflect on how that affects our lives.

We said earlier that the Liturgy of the Word is clearly a time of listening. Yet a visitor would have to be pardoned if he or she were confused about that point in many of our churches. So often we find people burying their heads in missalettes, reading along instead of focusing on the reader and listening to the Word as it is proclaimed. It often looks more like a joint reading or a classroom exercise than a time of listening. It is important to remember that this is a time for hearing what God has to say to us here and now, not a time for Bible study. It is helpful to read the readings before Mass begins so that they are familiar to us. Then during the proclamation we can sit back and listen, letting the Word strike us as God wills. Listening is an act of receptivity, a sign of openness and submissiveness. Having our own text in hand puts us, in a sense, in control of the Word. We can speed up, slow down, re-read, or skip over sections—we are in charge. But the attitude we need is the opposite—we are under the Word of God, submissive to whatever God has to say this day. The Word proclaimed is a living Word from a living Christ speaking through the reader. We should give him our undivided attention.

After the homily the whole assembly recites a profession of faith. This is the Nicene Creed, so called because it comes from the Council of Nicaea (325 A.D.), modified by the Council of Constantinople (381). This ancient profession stands as a response to God's Word, for our faith is always a response to what God has done. Having recalled God's wondrous works on our behalf in the readings, we profess our faith and trust.

As a further response, we join in the general intercessions. These prayers, offered for the needs of the Church and the world, are also called the prayer of the faithful, since they occur after the dismissal of the catechumens (those preparing for baptism), who were present for the Liturgy of the Word. Only the faithful (the baptized) properly join in the rest of the Eucharist.

The profession of faith and the general intercessions serve as a kind of transition from the entrance rite and the Liturgy of the Word to the Liturgy of the Eucharist and the dismissal.

Part III: The Sharing

A. The Preparation of the Gifts

After the general intercessions the congregation sits while the collection is gathered. Then the collection is brought forward, along with the bread and wine to be used in the Eucharistic meal. The bread and wine are placed on the altar table, and all is readied for the sacred meal. This action is easily recognized as setting the table for the meal. The preparation of the gifts is basically a functional section of the Mass in preparation for the Eucharistic meal.

The procession with the gifts and placing them on the altar are the oldest part of this section. In the early Church, after the gifts were presented the presider said a brief prayer over them, dedicating them for the sacrifice. Today that prayer is called the prayer over the gifts, and it is said at the end of the preparation rite. Through the centuries other rituals and prayers were added to this section, some of which were dropped in the revision of the Missal in 1970. Several minor rituals remaining in the current rite call for a bit of explanation.

When the chalice (cup) is prepared, a bit of water is mixed with the wine. It was the custom in ancient times, in religious rites and ordinary usage, to dilute the wine with water to make it less strong. Early Christians continued the custom in the Eucharist. That very practical action, however, was soon given symbolic meaning. In the West it came to represent the union of Christ with the faithful; just as the wine receives the water, so Christ takes us into himself and we are one with him. In the East the interpretation saw the wine and water as representing the divine and human natures of Christ. Just as one cannot separate the water and the wine, so Jesus is fully human and fully divine at one and the same time. In our current rite the silent prayer that accompanies this ritual gesture combines both interpretations: ''By the mystery of this water and wine may we come to share in the divinity of Christ, who humbled himself to share in our humanity.''

After the bread and cup have been prepared, the presider washes his hands. Like the mixing of the water and wine, this may originally have been a practical action following the presentation of the gifts when those gifts included various foods for the poor, etc. But washing hands as a sign of inner purity was customary both in Judaism and in early Christianity. It remains in the liturgy today as a reminder of our need to be cleansed from sin if we are to worship well. The silent prayer that accompanies this rite says: ''Lord, wash away my iniquity; cleanse me from my sin,'' a verse from Psalm 51.

During the collection and the procession with the gifts, a song may be sung. This is called the offertory song, which may be a bit confusing. This section of the Mass is not really an ''offertory'' in the sense of offering a sacrifice, but a preparation for the Eucharistic Prayer, in which the sacrifice of Christ is offered to the Father. The term ''offertory'' is a holdover from the Latin. The Latin word *offero* comes from *ob-fero*, which means ''to carry in front of''; it refers to bringing up the bread and wine. The song to accompany this procession with the gifts was called the *offertorium*, that is, the song that goes with bringing up the gifts. This procession with the gifts (God's gifts to us more than our gifts to God) is a symbol of our willingness to be involved in Christ's sacrifice. The bread and wine, ideally made by the local community, along with our monetary gifts, remind us of the call of Christ to give totally of ourselves in the service of others as he did. Thus we are prepared, along with the bread and wine, for the sacrificial meal to follow.

B. The Eucharistic Prayer

After the prayer over the gifts we begin the Eucharistic Prayer, the core of the Mass. This prayer derives from an ancient Jewish prayer form called *berakah*. The word *berakah* means "blessing," and it occurred in two forms. In the informal *berakah*, one blesses (praises and thanks) God with a fairly standard invocation (for example, "Blessed are you, Lord of creation") and then adds the reason ("for you have given us . . ."). The formal *berakah* begins the same way, but the reason is expanded to include a whole history of salvation. Intercessions are added that God will continue to bless us, and the prayer concludes with a final doxology, or blessing of God.

The Eucharistic Prayer has the same structure as the formal *berakah*, beginning with standard opening invocations of praise and thanks ("Let us give thanks to the Lord our God"); recalling God's wondrous works, especially in Jesus; offering petitions; and concluding with the doxology ("Through him, with him, in him . . ."). Eucharistic Prayer IV offers the clearest example of this structure, but all the Eucharistic Prayers contain the same elements.

After the preface that begins the Eucharistic Prayer, the congregation responds to this initial praise with the *Holy, holy, holy*. This hymn is drawn from Isaiah 6:2-3, which describes Isaiah's vision in the Temple. It was used in the Jewish liturgy even before its use in Christian worship, so it is one of the most ancient elements of the Mass. The second half of the text ("Blessed is he who comes . . .") is the acclamation used by the people during Christ's entry into Jerusalem (see Matthew 21:9).

After the *Holy, holy, holy* the Eucharistic Prayer continues with its memorial (*anamnesis* in Greek) of what God has done, focusing especially on the redemptive work of Jesus, including the account of the Last Supper. More than a mere "remembering," *anamnesis* involves the actual presence of God's saving deeds. That is the key to a proper understanding of the Mass as sacrifice. The sacrifice of Christ consists fundamentally in his total submission to the Father's will. That was expressed historically in his death-resurrection, but he remains forever in union with the Father's will. Thus he is forever priest and victim; his sacrifice is eternal. We can share in that one eternal sacrifice by uniting our wills with him in the Eucharist, since he is present among us, always offering himself to the Father. Christ's sacrifice becomes ours as well, as we are conformed to his image and committed to living out that sacrificial attitude in our daily lives as he did.

Through the power of the Holy Spirit, our *anamnesis* is an effective one. As we recall Christ's gift of himself at the Last Supper, he is present with us, offering himself again. We believe that the bread and wine are transformed into his body and blood, the fullest form of his presence among us. For centuries Christians of the West have focused on the words of institution ("This is my body . . . This is the cup of my blood") as the moment of consecration, while the Christians of the East have focused on the *epiclesis*, the prayer for the Holy Spirit, since it is by the power of the Holy Spirit that the transformation occurs. Liturgists and theologians today prefer not to try to isolate some "magic moment," but rather to see the whole Eucharistic Prayer as consecratory. The whole prayer is one *berakah*, one prayer of blessing over the bread and wine, and it is by this whole prayer of praise and thanks that the bread and wine are consecrated and changed into the body and blood of Christ.

After the institution narrative the congregation sings the memorial acclamation, which responds to the whole *anamnesis*, or memorial, that has been proclaimed. Then the prayer

continues, summing up the memorial and moving into petitions for God's continued blessings. It is noteworthy that the
first petition is always for the unity of the Church, usually men-
tioning the Holy Spirit as the source of that unity. This reminds
us that the whole purpose of the Eucharist is unity: unity between us and Christ, and unity with one another. Perhaps that
is why Christ chose a meal as the symbolic action for his sacrifice, since a meal is a very basic human symbol of unity.

After prayers for the living and the dead, the Eucharistic
Prayer includes a remembrance of the saints and prays that
we might share with them in the glory of Christ. Then the
prayer concludes with the final doxology and the Great Amen.
The word "Amen" is a short but important response to all that
has been proclaimed. Many people translate "Amen" as "So
be it," which is not a bad translation. Yet the word means a
lot more than that phrase seems to convey. Scholars tell us
that the root word in Hebrew from which "Amen" is derived
means "to pound in one's tent stake." Now that may not
sound too impressive until we recall that the people who used
that root word were desert nomads. One does not survive long
in the desert without a tent for protection from the heat of the
day and the cold of the night. Thus "to stake one's tent" comes
close to our expression "I'd stake my life on it!" That is really
the meaning of "Amen." It is a word that expresses commitment and agreement: "So be it in my life as I have just heard."
Our "Amen" at the end of the Eucharistic Prayer signifies our
acceptance of Jesus' way of life as our own, including his death
and resurrection. One might well hesitate to say "Amen"—
for such a short word it carries a lot of meaning and demands
much of those who say it.

C. The Communion Rite

At the Last Supper Jesus took bread and wine, said the
blessings, and gave them to the disciples. Our Eucharist fol-

lows the same pattern. After the preparation of the bread and wine and the proclamation of the blessing (*berakah*), we move into the communion rite, the sharing in the sacred meal. This rite begins with the Lord's Prayer, which has long been used as the table prayer for the Eucharist. It is especially appropriate, since it prays for our "daily bread" and asks for the forgiveness that is necessary for "communion" with all our brothers and sisters.

This second reason is also why the sign of peace occurs at this point in our Eucharist. It has been placed at various parts of the Mass in different areas and different centuries—at the beginning, after the penitential rite, before the gifts are prepared, etc. In our rite it occurs just before communion, because it signifies our willingness to be united in love and peace with one another, an essential attitude for those who share the one bread and one cup. In communion we express our deepest unity in Christ, so the sign of peace should help us to prepare properly. Not a greeting (we should do that when we arrive at church) or just a polite gesture, the sign of peace should be a prayerful wish that all our brothers and sisters will be blessed with *shalom*—that peace which includes all good things and is based on a right relationship with God and with all God's creation.

The breaking of the bread follows the sign of peace. This action, in preparation for sharing the one loaf, gave its name to the whole Eucharist in early times ("they gathered for the breaking of the bread"). It is a sign of our communion in the one Christ. As congregations grew larger, the breaking took some time, and the *Lamb of God* was sung to accompany this action. The General Instruction of the Roman Missal says that the eucharistic bread "should be made in such a way that the priest is able actually to break the host into parts and distribute them to at least some of the faithful . . . . The action of the breaking of the bread . . . will more clearly bring out the force and meaning of the sign of the unity of all in the one bread and of their charity, since the one bread is being distributed among the members of one family" (no. 283).

Sharing in communion is the climax of the Eucharist. Before we come to the table, we acknowledge our unworthiness ("Lord, I am not worthy . . .") and rejoice in the fact that God does not require us to be worthy but heals us by the divine Word. This is the same Jesus who scandalized the religious leaders of his time by sharing meals with sinners. He continues to do the same today. None of us are worthy of this meal; we share in it by God's gracious invitation.

Jesus told us to "Take and eat" and "Take and drink," and in recent years the Catholic Church has been moving toward regular sharing of both the bread and the cup. That was the practice for centuries, and to refuse the cup was seen as a sign of heresy. But by the fourteenth century, communion under the form of bread alone became more common for several reasons: concern about spilling, emphasis on seeing the host (the wine could not be seen as easily as the host in the monstrance), the new practice of kneeling for communion (making sharing the cup awkward), and the insistence against heretics that Christ was fully present under either the bread or the wine. Those concerns are no longer pressing issues, so the Second Vatican Council called for the restoration of the cup to the laity as a fuller sign of the meaning of the Eucharist and of Christ's total gift of himself to us.

When we receive the bread, the minister says "The body of Christ" and we answer "Amen." When we receive the cup, we also say "Amen" when the minister says "The blood of Christ." Our "Amen" at this point in the Mass is similar to the "Amen" at the end of the Eucharistic Prayer. It signifies our willingness to be the Body of Christ today, broken and shared with all, our willingness to be the Blood of Christ, poured out for the salvation of the world. To share in this sacrificial meal means accepting the mission of Christ today.

A communion song accompanies the reception of communion. It properly begins as the presider receives communion and continues until the end of the communion procession, when all have shared in the body and blood of the Lord. Singing at this time expresses the unity of the assembly as it shares in the sacrament of unity. In order for it to be sung easily, a song having a simple refrain for the assembly with verses sung by a cantor or choir is often chosen. After all have received and the song is finished, the whole assembly is seated for a time of silent prayer, communing with the Lord they have received. The communion rite then concludes with the prayer after communion.

Part IV: The Sending Forth

The dismissal rites of the Eucharist, like most leave-takings, are short and to the point. Originally the dismissal was simply a word to go forth, sometimes preceded by a blessing. It now includes the announcements, a greeting and blessing of the people, a formula of dismissal, the veneration of the altar, and the recessional hymn.

Any necessary announcements are made at the end of the Mass, since they concern the ways we carry out our mission as Christians after the Mass has ended. The whole dismissal rite is a rite of sending forth, a rite that commissions us to go forth to live the mystery we have celebrated in the Eucharist. The announcements remind us of various ways the community will seek to live the gospel during the coming week.

The blessing of the people is an ancient element of leave-taking. Fathers, when they left the house or went on a journey, blessed their children. Teachers blessed their students at the end of their lessons. And religious leaders blessed their congregations before they departed, asking God's care and guidance for them as they went forth to live their faith. The blessings used at Mass focus on a variety of God's gifts, often related to the day's theme.

The dismissal formula, as we noted earlier, gave the name "Mass" to the Eucharist. In Latin the formula was "Ite, missa est." The word *missa* was the technical word for dismissal, the conclusion of an official assembly. So the Latin phrase means "Go, it is the dismissal." But it also carries the sense of "Go, it is the sending" or "Go, you are sent." The early Church saw the Mass as extending into daily life. Strengthened by God's Word and nourished by the body and blood of Christ, the faithful were sent to proclaim that Word and to be the Body of Christ in the world. Perhaps it is because that sending forth was so important that it eventually gave its name to the whole celebration. It is to that sending forth that we joyfully respond, "Thanks be to God."

As the procession leaves the sanctuary, the presider again reverences the altar with a kiss as a sign of honor to Christ, and the procession leaves, often with a recessional hymn to accompany the movement. Thus the celebration ends, though its meaning and its effects are to continue through our daily lives until the next time we gather around the table of the Lord.

Some Final Reflections

Going step by step through the Mass as it is celebrated is a helpful way to understand the different parts of the ritual. It has the disadvantage, however, of making it difficult to see the overall rhythm that marks the celebration. Some parts are much more important than others, and some of the minor elements, because of their strangeness, require more explanation than the more important elements. In participating in the celebration, it is important to "go with the flow" of the natural rhythm of the ritual. That rhythm leads to a kind of peak at the gospel, the high point of the proclamation of the Word, then ebbs a bit through the preparation of the gifts. The Eucharistic Prayer is the central part of the Mass, a high plateau, as it were, with the sharing in communion following as a climactic point flowing from the Eucharistic Prayer. Then the ritual quickly tapers off to the dismissal, sending us forth renewed and recommitted.

The key to fruitful participation in the liturgy is to submit ourselves to it—to its rhythm, to the Word proclaimed, to Christ present, to the action of the Spirit. We are called to take an active role in the worship but are never in charge of it. The goal of worship is the human-divine encounter, and God is always in charge of that. To meet with the Eternal One, we can only open our hearts and prepare ourselves; we cannot make it happen. All too often we march through the liturgy, clergy and laity alike, as if we knew exactly what is going to happen; the net effect of that attitude is that nothing is likely to happen at all! God cannot be controlled or cornered. Our God is a God of surprises, and we had better be prepared to be surprised if we seek a meeting with the Holy One.

Another dimension of the openness we need is an openness to the power of symbols in worship. Ritual is a pattern of behavior based on symbols, which have a deep power to touch us and change us. In our society, with its pseudo-scientific bias, we have lost much of our sensitivity to the power of symbols. We need to reflect on the symbols we use in worship and try to experience them more fully. Eating a meal, bathing, rubbing with oil, laying a hand on the head, kneeling and bowing, processing and dancing are all symbolic activities that seek to engage us on multiple levels of our personalities. A full use of the symbols in our worship (e.g., plunging one's hand deeply into the holy water font to recall one's baptism, not just touching the surface with a finger), coupled with time spent in reflection outside the worship experience, could do much to deepen our awareness and our openness. Our religion is a symbolic one, an incarnational (enfleshed) faith. The more we open ourselves to the way God touches us through people and created things, the deeper our faith will grow.

Finally, it is important to remember that the liturgy is meant to be the source and summit of our spiritual life, not the whole of it. Good worship depends on regular prayer throughout the week. Our personal prayer life provides the basis we bring to the liturgy. There we join our experience of the Lord with the experiences of all the others who participate, and together we praise and thank the God who has touched and healed and saved each of us. The more we prepare, the more the liturgy will mean to us. And the more deeply we experience the liturgy, the more it will affect our daily life in the Lord. Christ calls us to his table and then sends us back out to continue his mission on earth. May these reflections help us all to live more fully in Christ Jesus, in worship and in daily life.

DISCUSSION/REFLECTION QUESTIONS

1. Is the four-part structure of the Mass evident in the celebration of the Sunday Eucharist in your parish? What would make it more obvious?

2. Do the gathering rites help you to feel a part of the assembly? How could they be improved?

3. Do the entrance rites help you prepare to listen to the Word of God? Would it be good to simplify this part of the Mass?

4. How effective is the proclamation of the Word of God in your parish? What can be done to improve the proclamation?

5. Are you generally able to listen well to the Word as it is proclaimed? What can you do to develop your listening skills?

6. Does the Jewish prayer-form *berakah* help you to understand the Eucharistic Prayer?

7. Does the sign of peace make you feel more united with the whole assembly as you prepare to receive communion?

8. Do you understand why the Church is restoring communion under both species (bread and wine) as the normal way of receiving communion? Is your parish moving in that direction?

9. Does the celebration of the Sunday Eucharist give you strength to live the gospel all week? Do you feel sent forth to be the Body of Christ when the assembly is dismissed?

10. How can you come to a deeper appreciation of the symbols we use in the Eucharist and in the other sacraments? Does your parish seem to be using those symbols more carefully and more richly today than in recent years?

11. Is the Eucharist the source and summit of your spiritual life? How are the Eucharist and your personal prayer life connected?

Sacraments of Healing

Chapter 4

PENANCE

Sacrament of Continuing Conversion

Did you know that
—penance could be received only once in a lifetime in the early Church?
—at one time the Church had a two-track system of public penance and private penance?
—penance and confession are not exactly the same thing?
—for centuries it was required that penitents do their assigned penance and then return to receive absolution?
—that many Christians in the past confessed their sins to lay persons?
—the first confessionals were not built in the carpenter shop of Joseph and Jesus?

These and many other interesting facts about the sacrament of penance are revealed by a study of the history of this sacrament. That history makes it clear that penance has had a very lively and varied past. Unfortunately it does not seem to have a very lively present, since many Catholics seem to have abandoned this sacrament completely, while others seem very confused about the value and proper role of penance in the spiritual life of the ordinary Christian. This chapter is designed

71

to explore the possibilities for penance in the future of the Church and to examine how this sacrament can be better understood and renewed within the community of Christians.

A Look at History

An understanding of the history of penance is a good place to begin to understand both its proper meaning and the possibilities for its future. We find very little about penance in the New Testament, though it is clear that the Church was given the power to forgive sin. We have no record of how penance was celebrated, if in fact it was celebrated at all as a special sacrament in the New Testament period. The main celebration of forgiveness of sin in the New Testament Church was baptism. That was the sacrament of forgiveness that brought salvation, and it was almost unthinkable that those who had been converted to Christ and abandoned their old life of sin would return to sin after they had been baptized. "How can we who died to sin go on living in it?" Paul asks. "This we know: our old self was crucified with him so that the sinful body might be destroyed and we might be slaves to sin no longer. . . . you must consider yourselves dead to sin but alive for God in Christ Jesus" (Rom 6:2, 6, 11).

Nevertheless, the Church soon found out that it had to deal with post-baptismal sin, with Christians who slipped back into a sinful life after their initial conversion and baptism. Since the early Christians saw that as a need for re-conversion, it was natural that the shape of the sacrament of penance was modeled on the catechumenate, the process of preparation for baptism. They called penance a "second baptism," noting that the first baptism was with water, while the second was with tears. A Christian who slipped back into a sinful life apparently had not properly converted the first time. So the sacrament of penance was designed to foster conversion in much the same way as the catechumenate did for those preparing for baptism. (See pp. 15–16 for a description of the ancient catechumenate.)

The order of penitents

When the Church wanted to foster re-conversion in those who had fallen into serious post-baptismal sin, it naturally patterned the process after the catechumenate. As those preparing for baptism formed the order of catechumens, those preparing for "second baptism" formed the order of penitents. The penitents first confessed their sins to the bishop or his designated representative. It is generally agreed that this confession was done privately, but that was the only part of the sacrament that was private.

After the confession the penitents were enrolled in the order of penitents, often with the imposition of ashes. While they were in the order of penitents, they carried out whatever penances had been assigned by the confessor. Those penances were often very long and severe, sometimes lasting several years. During that time the penitents usually had special places in church, often wore special garments, and commonly left the Eucharist after the homily, just as the catechumens did. When the penance had been completed and conversion was judged to have occurred, the penitents were welcomed back into the order of the faithful with a rite of reconciliation. That was celebrated by the whole community, often on Holy Thursday, with the imposition of hands by the bishop and readmittance to the Eucharistic table. Commonly, however, the reconciled penitents were expected to continue penitential practices (such as abstinence from sexual intercourse) for the rest of their lives.

A person could be admitted into the order of penitents only once in his or her lifetime in the early Church. It was not required for all sins, and the most common list of sins requiring that discipline included murder, adultery, and apostasy (renunciation of the faith). Lesser sins were understood to be forgiven through prayer, personal penance, almsgiving, and the celebration of the Eucharist. Those who sinned seriously, though, were given one opportunity to re-convert. If they sinned again after that, the Church left them to the mercy of God. God could always forgive again, but the Church felt it could not or should not admit penitents to the order of penitents a second time. That indicates a constant concern of the early Church not to encourage sin by being too lenient with sinners.

Partly because it was restricted to once in a lifetime and partly because it was such a strict and demanding discipline, the order of penitents was not too popular. Eventually it began to decline and was used rarely, and then usually only at the point of death (thus minimizing the lifetime penances expected of the reconciled). By about the seventh and eighth centuries, it was obvious that the order of penitents was not adequate to deal with the need for forgiveness of many of the faithful.

Irish private penance

About that time the Irish monks came to the Continent to convert the Franco-Germanic tribes. They brought with them a different form of the celebration of penance that had developed in their homeland. The Church in Ireland was organized around the monasteries, and this new form of penance probably developed in connection with the monastic practice of admitting one's faults to the abbot for spiritual guidance. The Irish practice of penance was generally private, celebrated between the confessor and penitent. It could be repeated often in one's life, according to need. However, it would not have been celebrated too frequently, for the penances were still very strict and often long-lasting.

It seems that this Irish form of confession originally had no formal rite of reconciliation or absolution. After it became popular, the Church adopted this form and added a ritual expression of absolution. For a while the traditional order of the sacrament was followed. After confessing his or her sins, the penitent was assigned a penance, which had to be completed before returning to the confessor to receive absolution. Practical difficulties with this order became apparent when the confessor was a wandering missionary and when the penances often took the penitent on pilgrimage to foreign lands. It was often difficult, if not impossible, to return later to seek absolution. Therefore confessors began to give absolution at the time of confession; the penance would be completed later.

The demise of public penance

For a while those two types of penance coexisted in the Church, and it became a common rule that public sins required public penance (the order of penitents), while private sins could be forgiven through private penance. This two-track system, however, eventually fell into disuse because of the reluctance of penitents to enter the very demanding order of penitents. The severity of the penances in the Irish form of the sacrament was also lessened over time. The first step was the development of substitutions. The penances were commonly determined by recourse to books known as Penitentials. These books listed an appropriate penance for each sin committed, and if someone had committed a large number of sins, the total penance could exceed the practical possibilities of a lifetime (e.g., years of fasting, pilgrimages to Jerusalem, etc.). In such cases, substitutions were made, often of certain prayers or almsgiving that took the place of the assigned penances. From that developed the practice of indulgences, by which certain prayers or pious practices were considered equivalent to so many days of penance (not days in purgatory, as many have wrongly understood).

With less severe penances and more frequent celebration, the sacrament of penance took on a form very similar to our twentieth-century experience. Two important additions to the tradition of this sacrament occurred around the time of the Council of Trent in the sixteenth century. The Council required that serious sins be confessed according to number and kind of sin. That led in later years to what has been called the "grocery list" approach to the sacrament, that is, listing all sins, mortal or venial, by kind and number. It was also after Trent that it became customary to celebrate the sacrament of penance in a confessional box set aside for that purpose.

There was little change in the form of penance between the Council of Trent and the Second Vatican Council (1962–65). There was considerable change, however, in the approach to this sacrament taken by the majority of Catholics. The seventeenth-century movement known as Jansenism had a significant effect on popular piety, an effect that has continued until recent years. Jansenism stressed the deep unworthiness of human beings to approach God and urged infrequent communion, which was always to be preceded by the sacrament of penance.

The twentieth century

In contrast, at the beginning of this century Pope Pius X promoted more frequent reception of communion and moved the age of first communion from fourteen to around seven. Since the link between penance and communion was very strong at that time, first confession was also moved to age seven.

Changes in sacramental practice usually take a long time, and the efforts of Pope Pius X only reached their fruition in the 1950s and 1960s. At the same time, reception of the sacrament of penance also became much more frequent. The pontificate of Pope Pius XII, in the 1940s and 1950s, saw the most frequent use of this sacrament in the whole history of the Church. It is important for us to realize that this period, which seems normal to many in the Church today, was really an un-usual time in the overall history of the sacrament of penance.

In the 1960s and 1970s the frequent use of penance began to decline rapidly. One of the most frequent reasons given for the sudden drop has been a shift in Catholics' sense of sin. Some see it as a denial of the very reality of sin, but more often, it seems, the shift is a movement away from an overemphasis on sexual morality above all other moral issues, from a taboo understanding of sin as a breaking of an absolute law, and from a purely private morality that tended to ignore areas like racial sins and economic injustice. Catholics have begun to understand sin in a more personal and broader way, and their prior experience of penance seems to many to be linked to the older view of morality. For many, confession was a ritual act with little relationship to spiritual growth or conversion. It was required in order to avoid the flames of hell and promised "grace" to help avoid sin in the future; yet that grace did not seem to work, for people frequently complained of confessing the same sins over and over with little sense of growth.

Moreover, for many Catholics the sacrament of penance had become a rather negative experience, in which the sense of guilt was much stronger than the sense of God's mercy and forgiveness. One went to confession as a punishment rather than as a celebration. That all fit together when religion was understood primarily as a matter of following rules and earning one's way to heaven. When Catholics began to recover the traditional sense of God's love and mercy and the free gift of grace (which we can never earn by being good), the sacrament of penance ceased to make sense to many of those who had been regular penitents.

The Revised Rites of Reconciliation

The Second Vatican Council called for a revision of the rites of penance. The new rites, which were issued in 1969, consist of three forms of reconciliation. The first form, for individual confession, has been falsely described as just the same as confession before the Council. In fact, the first form is intended to be a much richer and more personal experience. It is to include the reading of Scripture, reminding us of God's mercy, and it is supposed to be a time of shared conversation and prayer between the priest and penitent. The details of the ritual are less important than the overall experience that is intended. This form of the rite is designed to provide the opportunity to probe one's life and to seek spiritual growth with the aid of a skilled confessor.

The second form, which places individual reconciliation in the context of a communal penance service, does not envision the leisure to engage in any extensive dialogue. The encounter with the confessor must necessarily be brief due to the numbers involved, but this second form emphasizes the communal nature of our sins and our reconciliation.

The third form, with general absolution, is currently restricted to unusual situations in which it is not possible to offer individual reconciliation. When this form is celebrated, those persons with serious sins are expected to seek out a confessor at a later time to confess their sins individually.

Despite the introduction of these revised rites, the individual celebration of penance has continued to decline. Many parishes find today that people will come in significant numbers to celebrate a communal penance service, with or without individual reconciliation, for Lent and Advent, while the weekly confession times bring few penitents. There have been various attempts, both local and worldwide, to encourage the use of this sacrament, but they seem to have had minimal effect.

Gleanings from History

The point of studying history is not to return to some ideal time of the past, but to see what the past can teach us about the meaning of penance and the dynamics that can make it a helpful part of the Christian life. Even this brief historical overview reveals several important insights.

A community sacrament

One of the most basic insights is that the sacrament of penance, like all sacraments, has a fundamental community dimension. That was more obvious in the early Church, with the order of penitents and its public character, but even with the later private penance the Church has always insisted on the importance of the priest in the experience of reconciliation, not because God will not forgive us directly (God always forgives those who repent), but because the priest is the representative of the Church community. Reconciliation with the Church community is the sacramental sign of reconciliation with the Lord. The priest is the representative of the community, which is the Body of Christ. He is also the representative of Christ, but his community role is fundamental.

The renewed rites of penance have given many Catholics a sense of the community dimension of the sacrament through communal penance services. Yet the role of the community is still weak and poorly understood for the most part. The community is basic to the celebration of any sacrament. Sacraments are celebrations by the community of the work of God's grace in the individuals or group around whom the sacraments are celebrated. In baptism the community celebrates the initiation of new members into the Church and God's grace at work in those new members. In marriage the community gathers to celebrate the love of God as it is revealed in the love of husband and wife. In penance the community celebrates the forgiveness of God and the conversion of life that the Holy Spirit is accomplishing in the lives of the penitents.

That community dimension is not something just added on to what is fundamentally a private matter. It is basic to the very notion of sacrament as the community's celebration. A renewed understanding of the communal sense of all the sacraments is essential to the renewal of the sacraments decreed by the Second Vatican Council. It is perhaps most essential for the sacrament of penance, since this sacrament has had the least communal form of celebration in the recent past.

A process of conversion

What the community celebrates in penance is conversion, and the centrality of conversion to the experience of this sacrament is the second thing we can learn from its history. Christ preached a message that called people to reform their lives and believe in the Good News (see Mark 1:15). That call to reform and believe is an invitation to conversion. Our lives must be converted from sin and selfishness to love and holiness. The Catholic Church has always understood conversion as a process that occurs over time. There may be significant moments within that process, moments that can be called "the day of conversion," but even fundamentalist revival preachers recognize that such moments must be supported and affirmed by ongoing growth in Christ.

The most basic conversion is that initial turning to Christ that is celebrated in baptism. If the one baptized is an adult, the Church looks for evidence of conversion before baptism is celebrated. The catechumenate is the process by which the Christian community seeks to foster the conversion of adult candidates. If the one baptized is an infant, the conversion process must be fostered by the family and the Church community as the child grows and matures. But after the initial conversion journey, much still remains to be done. The journey of conversion is a lifetime one, as we seek to give our lives more and more to Christ. Penance is the sacrament that celebrates that ongoing conversion.

The awareness of conversion as a process is also important for our understanding of the sacrament of penance itself. Every sacrament requires a process, within which the sacrament is a moment that celebrates what has been going on in that process and propels those who celebrate to continue in the same process. In penance the process is one of conversion. The sacrament celebrates the conversion that has been occurring and fosters a continuing conversion following the celebration.

The emphasis on conversion in the history of penance also helps us to grapple with the question of frequency of celebrating the sacrament. It is generally not helpful to establish some arbitrary schedule of celebration based on the calendar (e.g., every week or every month). It is appropriate to celebrate penance whenever there is a significant experience of conversion to celebrate. If there is no conversion occurring, the celebration of the sacrament becomes an empty exercise. This does not mean that penance can only be celebrated when the movement of conversion is complete, but the process must be underway. Sometimes a person may sense God's call to change but be unsure just what the change entails. At other times one might be very clear about the direction God wants but be hesitant to make the commitment to change. At still other times the change may be well underway, and the sacrament celebrates what is largely accomplished already. The sacrament could well be celebrated at any of those moments, as long as there is some conversion experience to celebrate.

It is also important to recognize that these two issues, community and conversion, are intimately related. The conversion to which we are called is precisely a conversion to a fuller life in the community of the Church. Too often we think of conversion or spiritual growth as a private matter between God and the individual; but God calls us into community, and true spiritual growth will lead us to a deeper relationship and commitment to the life and mission of the Church.

Moreover, conversion takes place within the community and with the prayers and support of other members of the Church. Many people who have begun to experience a deep sense of community in the Church, often in small groups of Christians studying or praying or working together, have discovered how much help in living the gospel comes from the support of other Christians. Though that community involvement and support have been minimal in recent centuries, the revised rites of penance are designed to help us recover a sense of conversion within, and reconciliation to, the Church community.

Elements of the Sacraments

It is also apparent from history that there are three basic elements to the sacrament of penance: confession, penance, and absolution or reconciliation. These elements have been arranged in different orders at different times, but all three seem to be essential. In the early Church the order was always confession, penance, and then absolution. Soon after the Irish form was adopted, the order changed to confession, absolution, and then penance. And with the third form of the current rites, the one with general absolution, we have absolution, penance, and then confession. (If there are serious sins, a penitent must seek out a confessor when possible after the celebration of general absolution.)

The confession

The three elements of confession, penance, and absolution each witness to a different dynamic of the conversion process. The one most people, Catholic and non-Catholic, associate with the sacrament of penance is confession. At different times in our history the Church has understood the importance of confession in various ways. Originally confession referred to an act of praise of God, confessing what God had done in one's life by the grace of conversion. The telling of one's sins was secondary; what God was doing was primary.

Another approach sees the confession as an act of penance in itself, involving personal admission of guilt and a humbling of self. It was this understanding that gave rise to the practice of lay confession when a priest was not available. That may not have been understood precisely as a sacrament, but confession alone was seen as effective in achieving reconciliation, since it was an act of repentance that atoned for sin.

A third approach sees confession as simply practical. If the priest is to function as a judge (a common image in the past), he must know the nature of the crime before he imposes punishment. That courtroom image is no longer popular, but the approach still has some validity in that the priest does need to know what areas of conversion are at issue if he is to help foster that conversion process.

This is perhaps the most helpful understanding of confession—as an aid to the conversion of the penitent. The personal encounter with the confessor provides a forum in which the penitent can be honest with self and with God. Simply expressing one's current condition often helps to clarify the areas that need conversion and to make the necessary commitment to change. Moreover, the confessor should be one who is skilled in guiding people through the conversion journey and offering spiritual direction. It is the value of this personal encounter for conversion that makes sense of the Vatican's insistence that confession should be undertaken even when one has already been absolved through general absolution.

The penance

In the early Church it was doing the penance that was seen as the central element of the sacrament. The working out of a penance was understood as conversion therapy, fostering the real change of life that penance required. The centrality of this element is indicated by the fact that it gave its name to the whole sacrament, just as a later age would come to call it simply "confession."

In the Middle Ages the doing of the penance was commonly understood as necessary for the removal of the temporal punishment due to sin. This understanding was fostered by the fact that absolution was granted before the penance was done. Thus forgiveness was already assured, and the penance was seen to deal with the effects of sin that were not removed by forgiveness. The central point of that approach is valid, even if the language does not find ready acceptance today. Though God forgives us freely and completely, sin affects us in ways that must be undone over time. If I have been selfish, I need to grow in my ability to love, and the penance should help me to do that. That insight has led most confessors today to try to suggest penances that match the area of conversion with which the particular penitent is struggling. Sometimes that may be prayer, but the old standard of "three Our Fathers and three Hail Marys" is often not the best penance. The penance should help the penitent to grow in precisely the areas that God is calling him or her to change.

The reconciliation

The third element, absolution, is also called reconciliation, and thus has given its name to the whole sacrament in the revised rites (which call it the sacrament of reconciliation or penance). This element focuses on the action of God, who absolves us and reconciles us. At the same time, since the reconciling work of God is today the work of the Church, it also focuses on the action of the Church in reconciling penitents to the community and thus to the Lord.

Reconciliation is the basis for the celebration of the sacrament. It is precisely this element that is cause for joy and celebration, and in the early Church the Holy Thursday ritual of reconciliation was the richest part of the sacrament. The new rites of penance encourage renewed attention to this part of the sacrament, especially in the second and third forms of the sacrament, which involve communal celebrations of the reconciling grace of God.

Celebrating Reconciliation Well

Fruitful celebration of the sacrament of reconciliation today can be fostered by careful attention to all three of these elements of the sacrament. All the sacraments have suffered through the centuries from a tendency to reduce them to the bare minimum necessary. The renewal of these central rituals of our faith requires a fuller experience of the richness of the sacraments revealed by their history. That is certainly true of the sacrament of penance, for our recent celebrations of this sacrament have barely hinted at the richness of its past or its potential for the future. The rites for the celebration of reconciliation have been revised to express more of that richness. What is even more important is that we renew our approach to the sacrament in a way that will enable us to experience it more fully and deeply.

Our understanding of the confession of sins, for example, would benefit greatly if we recovered a sense of praise as primary. We confess what God is doing in our lives and how divine grace has led us to recognize our need for conversion. In that context we share with the confessor the current state of our relationship with God and the Church. That includes admitting our sins, but it also requires a deeper examination of why we do those things, of the underlying attitudes and desires that express themselves in our sinful actions. At the same time, a good confession should also focus on how God's grace is being experienced and what growth God has been fostering in one's life. In short, our confession should be an expression of where we are in our continual journey of conversion to Christ's way of life.

A much more serious approach to penance as an element of this sacrament can be very helpful in making it a richer experience. In recent centuries the element of penance has been minimized, and for many people it has been a mere footnote to the sacrament, something to be done in a couple of minutes before leaving the church building. But the penance is meant to be a central aid in changing our lives, in fostering true conversion. Doing penance really means the hard work of changing the way we think and feel and act. That takes time, whether we do it before we approach the sacrament, after we have been reconciled, or in the process of an experience of the sacrament extended over a period of time. We need to ask ourselves what practical steps we need to take to make a real change in the way we live. We might suggest those practical steps to our confessor or ask him for guidance in deciding how to further our conversion. Even if we are given another, simpler penance to do, we can always add to that whatever we know would really help us to change. That would go a long way toward meeting one of the most common complaints about our past use of this sacrament, namely, that it does not seem to make any difference in our lives.

Reconciliation, too, needs to be understood more deeply. A first step, perhaps, is to see it more as reconciliation than absolution. Absolution suggests a cleansing and a freeing from sin, an official declaration of forgiveness. But the sacrament finds its special role in the Church's life precisely in the realm of reconciliation. God's forgiveness is available to us in many ways. The sacrament celebrates the healing of relationships not only with God but also with the community of the Church. It is here that the sacramental symbol lies: reconciliation with the Church is the effective sign of reconciliation with God. That includes forgiveness, of course, but reconciliation is a broader and richer reality, focusing directly on the relationships that are being healed through God's grace. When we approach the sacrament, we need to remember that we are seeking a deeper union both with God and with God's people.

That is perhaps the most important dimension of the sacrament of reconciliation that we need to recover—it is radically a communal celebration. It reintegrates us into the community when we have severed our bonds through serious sin, and it strengthens those bonds when they have been weakened by lesser sins. Much of the neglect of this sacrament in our own time seems to stem from the realization that God will forgive us in many ways besides the sacrament of reconciliation. Some falsely conclude, therefore, that there is no need for the sacrament. That indicates how much we need a renewal of our sense of identity as a community of God's people. We are saved in community, not in isolation. By our baptism we were incorporated into that community of faith, and our belonging brings a responsibility to carry on the work of the community. When we realize how deeply our identity in Christ is bound up with our brothers and sisters in faith, the importance of reconciliation with those brothers and sisters will be obvious.

An Order of Penitents

Various scholars and pastoral workers have begun to advocate a further revision of the rites of penance to foster a deeper renewal of this sacrament. A number of their suggestions revolve around the re-establishment of the order of penitents in a modern form. Like the ancient order, this form of the sacrament would be extended over time, would involve the whole community, and would be geared to fostering a deep conversion. Unlike the old order, it would be open to others besides serious sinners, it could be celebrated more than once in a lifetime, and it would probably be much shorter and less demanding than the lifetime penances of the past.

The introduction of an order of penitents would have been unthinkable even to the scholars a few years ago. Recent experience with the RCIA and the catechumenate, however, has shown the viability of having a small group of people within a parish who publicly witness to their conversion process and invite the whole community to support them in their journey. In fact, the introduction of the catechumenate in many parishes has led directly to pastoral experiments with an order of penitents, because some of those who are already baptized have asked for an experience similar to the catechumenate to deepen their own conversion. An order of penitents is precisely such a process.

Those who envision such an order suggest that it might begin on Ash Wednesday, with entrance into the order marked by the ancient symbol of ashes. The penitents would have already met with a confessor and been assigned a penance, which they would carry out during Lent. They might also meet with the confessor or another spiritual director periodically during Lent to reflect on the progress of their conversion and to adjust the penance if necessary. After completing their assigned penance, the penitents would be reconciled with the community in a special ceremony on Holy Thursday. This fuller form of the sacrament might be especially helpful to those who have been living in serious sin and need a deep conversion, to those who have been away from the Church for a long period of time and need to re-enter gradually, and to those who sense a call from God to a deeper level of conversion and the need for an extended time to work through that conversion process. Those who would enter the order of penitents would probably be few in number, but they would stand as a living witness to the whole community of the call to conversion and the importance of penance in the Christian way of life.

Some parishes have already begun to experiment with such an order of penitents, and the future may see this idea spread.

Cardinal Joseph Bernardin suggested the revival of the order of penitents at the Synod of Bishops in 1983, but no official response to this suggestion was forthcoming from the Vatican.

Even if one's parish does not start a formal order of penitents, however, keeping the model in mind can still help us to renew our personal approach to this sacrament. It can remind us that we must always provide for a process of conversion when we celebrate penance. That means taking time and paying attention to the promptings of the Spirit of God in our own lives. It also means taking seriously the penance assigned in the sacrament so that it can be a means of furthering our own conversion.

This model can also help us to understand conversion as the core of Christian life and the importance of constantly seeking to deepen our own conversion, turning our life over to Christ more and more. Such awareness can help us to decide when it is appropriate to celebrate the sacrament of penance, that is, whenever we are aware of a significant call from the Lord and are ready to respond to that call.

This model can also help us to deepen our understanding of the role of the community in our whole spiritual life, a community that is affected by every sin we commit and that is involved in every celebration of reconciliation.

Finally, the model of the order of penitents can help us to understand better the way penance and Lent are linked. The whole Church celebrates penance during Lent because penance is a "second baptism," and Lent is a time for baptismal renewal. That does not mean, however, that every member of the parish must celebrate the sacrament individually. Just as the whole congregation celebrates a wedding even though only two persons are getting married, so the whole Church can celebrate penance even if only a few members are actually going through an order of penitents.

Conclusion

It should be clear by now that the sacrament of penance has had quite a varied history, with different forms, places, frequency, and emphasis. The Church has always been willing to adapt the sacrament to meet the needs and spirit of the times, but she has never been willing to give it up, for it is too important for the life and growth of true followers of Christ.

No one can predict with certainty just how this sacrament will develop in the future. Its shape and use will be determined in practice as the Church lives its life and seeks to follow its Lord. Each of us must discover what the future of penance is for ourselves, and all of us together must determine its future in the life of the Church. May the Spirit of the Lord guide us to a healthy use of this sacrament that will move us all further along the road to full conversion in Christ Jesus.

DISCUSSION/REFLECTION QUESTIONS

1. What was the most surprising thing to you in the history of the sacrament of penance?

2. Does the history of the order of penitents help you to understand the purpose and meaning of this sacrament?

3. Could an order of penitents be workable in your parish today? What attitudes would have to change, and what else would have to happen for it to work?

4. What do you think is the reason so few Catholics make use of this sacrament today?

5. Why do you think so many people have such negative memories of penance? Were that many priests poor confessors, or do people have unrealistic expectations of confessors? Or do they just remember one negative experience forever?

6. How many of the three forms of the new rites of reconciliation have you experienced? Which was the most helpful to you? Why?

7. How can we recover a deeper sense of the communal dimension of reconciliation? What would be the first step in your parish?

8. Do you see conversion as the basic dynamic of your life in Christ? In what ways is God calling you to a deeper conversion at this point in your life? Can the sacrament of reconciliation be helpful in that conversion process?

9. How can you personally come to a deeper experience of the richness of confession, of penance, and of reconciliation?

10. How can children be led to a healthy appreciation of this sacrament?

Chapter 5

ANOINTING
Sacrament of the Sick

It was so common that it almost became a cliché in books and movies. "Oh, they've called for the priest. There's no hope now." Calling for the priest was seen as the kiss of death. It was put off until the last possible moment, lest the arrival of the priest actually hasten death by frightening the patient. The priest's arrival for the "last rites" was a sign of doom. When the doctors could do no more, it was time to call the priest. It was truly "extreme unction," delayed until death was extremely close.

One might assume that such a scenario was a fictional exaggeration, but it was very close to reality for many Catholics in the recent past. I was ordained the same year that the new Rite of Anointing and Pastoral Care of the Sick was issued from Rome (1972), and I remember the difficulty of suggesting to a family that we celebrate this sacrament for their loved one. Such a suggestion was often rejected, because to agree to the anointing was to give up hope and face the imminence of death.

Fortunately that attitude is fading today in light of the reform of the sacraments mandated by the Second Vatican Council. People are beginning to see this sacrament more as a sacrament of the sick than as last rites for the dying. Many Catholics, of course, still view the coming of the priest with fear and trembling, retaining the old perspective of anointing as "extreme unction." And many others, though they know that the old views have changed somehow, are not sure what this sacrament means today or when it should be celebrated.

The confusion is understandable, for the Second Vatican Council and the subsequent reform of the sacraments have made a significant shift in our understanding of the sacrament of anointing. The Council noted that this sacrament may "more fittingly be called 'Anointing of the Sick'" and stressed that it is not reserved only to those who are at the point of death (Constitution on the Liturgy, no. 73). That marked the beginning of a recovery of the original understanding of this sacrament, a process that has been furthered by the new Rite for Anointing issued in 1972. It is no longer called extreme unction or the last rites but anointing of the sick, and the shift in name indicates a vast shift in both pastoral practice and the theology of the sacrament.

Such a shift in understanding, however, does not take root in the Church simply by papal decrees and official rites. Many today still fear this sacrament, while others have begun to look more to charismatic healers for help in dealing with illness. There is clearly a need for a deeper understanding of the true purpose of this sacrament and the wider pastoral care that the Church can offer to those who are ill.

A Look at History

Since the recent reforms of this sacrament are really a recovery of its original purpose, it will be helpful to take a look at the development of the anointing of the sick in the history of the Church. Actually, anointing is older than the Church itself, since it was a commonly used ritual in the Old Testament.

Kings, priests, and prophets were anointed as a sign of their special mission and the gift of God's spirit to help them. Similarly, various objects used in worship were consecrated by anointing. Oil was also used for treating wounds, healing the sick, and preparing the dead for burial. It was an item in common use in the ancient world, employed in such diverse activities as cooking, athletic rub-downs, cosmetics, and lighting. Because of its many uses, it came to symbolize various meanings, which are retained when oil is used in ritual activities. Thus the use of oil speaks of strength and health, of light and beauty, of consecration and God's spirit.

It is not surprising, then, that Jesus and his followers also made use of oil in religious ways. Two references to anointing the sick in the New Testament have been influential in the history of the sacrament. The first is Mark 6:13, which reads, "They expelled many demons, anointed the sick with oil and worked many cures." That was part of the disciples' ministry of preaching and healing, an extension of Jesus' own ministry.

The more influential passage, however, comes from the Letter of James, which places care of the sick in the context of other pastoral situations: "If anyone among you is suffering hardship, he must pray. If a person is in good spirits, he should sing a hymn of praise. Is there anyone sick among you? He should ask for the presbyters of the church. They in turn are to pray over him, anointing him with oil in the Name of the Lord. This prayer uttered in faith will reclaim the one who is ill, and the Lord will restore him to health. If he has committed any sins, forgiveness will be his. Hence, declare your sins to one another, and pray for one another, that you may find healing" (5:13-16).

Several points are worth noting here. James speaks specifically of the presbyters, who were the leaders of the community, the council of elders. Presbyters later became known as priests, and this passage is no doubt the basis for the later restriction of anointing to ordained priests. James also stresses the importance of the prayer of faith. It is this prayer that will save the sick man. Finally, it is important to note the mingling of healing and forgiveness in this passage, which gives a hint of the wholistic perspective of the early Church. Care of the sick was directed to the whole person. Both physical and spiritual healing were sought, for the ancient world saw a close connection between spiritual, mental, and physical health, a perspective that modern medical science is beginning to recover.

The first eight hundred years

The history of this sacrament can be divided into two major periods. For the first eight centuries of the Church's life, one perspective prevailed. Then, following the Carolingian reforms of the ninth century, a different perspective became dominant and prevailed until the reforms of the Second Vatican Council (1962–65).

In the first eight hundred years the sacrament was clearly seen as a rite for the sick. There is almost no mention of the use of the anointing for those who were dying. Anointing was a sacrament of healing and part of the Church's normal care of the sick. The liturgical books show a great concern for the blessing of the oil by the bishop but offer no evidence of a formal rite for doing the anointing. The blessing strengthened the oil with divine power; who actually applied the oil to the sick person was not that important. Certainly it was appropriate for the bishop himself to do so, but if it was not possible for the bishop to visit all the sick regularly, then the sick could be anointed by a presbyter (priest) or by a lay person. There is even indication that sometimes the sick could anoint themselves with the holy oil. The oil was applied in various ways, often by anointing the afflicted part of the body. Sometimes the oil was apparently taken internally like medicine, though external use was more common.

In that early period there was more stress on the bodily effects of the anointing than on the spiritual effects. This was a sacrament of healing, and it was intended for the care of the sick, not the dying. At the same time, there was still that wholistic approach to healing which recognized that body and spirit are not separate entities and that God came to save the whole person. The sacrament, therefore, was intended to promote wholeness of body and mind and soul and spirit. That could involve physical healing, forgiveness of sin, strengthening of the spirit, calming of mental distress, or any combination of these effects that the sick person needed.

From Charlemagne to Vatican II

In the ninth century the emperor Charlemagne supported a major reform of the liturgical rites of the Church within his realm. He sought a uniformity of Church worship to unify his kingdom. This Carolingian reform had a great impact on the practice of anointing. It restricted the anointing with oil to presbyters (priests) and bishops, so that lay people could no longer anoint themselves or their sick relatives. The reform also produced a full ritual for how the anointing was to be done.

At that same time the anointing began to be associated with the rites for the dying, viaticum (communion for the dying) and deathbed reconciliation. Because the sacrament of penance could be received only once in the early Church, it had become common to put it off until the moment of death. Since this sacrament had to be celebrated by the ordained clergy, and since it was customary that the anointing could not be given to penitents until they had been reconciled, it was natural that the anointing, now also restricted to the clergy, would become part of the deathbed ministry. The sequence soon became penance, followed by anointing, and concluding with viaticum. In the twelfth century the order was changed to penance, viaticum, and anointing, which reinforced the idea that anointing was "extreme unction," the last anointing *"in extremis,"* at the moment of death.

As the anointing of the sick became extreme unction, there was a natural change in focus concerning the effects of the sacrament. Usually the sick person was dying when the sacrament was celebrated, so physical healing was not generally experienced or expected. The emphasis shifted more and more to purely spiritual effects, especially the forgiveness of sins and preparation for the beatific vision.

The great Scholastic theologians, reflecting on the common practice of this sacrament in their own time, explained it as a sacrament for the dying. They debated about the precise effects of the anointing, some teaching that it removed venial sins, while others insisted that it removed the remnants of sin which remained after forgiveness and which would prevent entrance into the beatific vision. But both groups saw it as resulting in forgiveness to prepare those who were dying for entry into heaven. And so it became common to insist that the sacrament could not be received until death was imminent.

The Council of Trent (1545–63) took place after several centuries of such practice and theory. Surprisingly, however, the Council refrained from ratifying the stress on anointing as a sacrament of the dying. The Council said, instead, that the anointing was to be administered to the sick, especially to those who were dangerously ill and seemed near death. Thus the Council left the door open for the reforms of the Second Vatican Council in our own time, which restored the sacrament as a sacrament for the sick, not just for the dying.

Those recent reforms became obvious with the change of the name from extreme unction to anointing of the sick. The Council also urged an earlier use of the sacrament, noting that it should be administered at the very beginning of the danger of death from sickness or old age. The bishops also restored the order of the sacraments for the dying to penance, anointing, and viaticum.

The Current Rites

The rite prepared by the Congregation for Divine Worship to carry out the Council's reforms places the sacramental ministry in the context of a wider pastoral care of the sick. The rite itself was originally called "The Rite of Anointing and Pastoral Care of the Sick." The final version of the rite in this country makes the context even clearer, carrying the title "Pastoral Care of the Sick: Rites of Anointing and Viaticum."

The introduction to the rite highlights the role of the whole Christian community in caring for the sick. Doctors and other health-care personnel share in the ministry in their own special roles. All baptized Christians are urged to participate in the ministry to the sick, offering them their love and care and celebrating the sacraments with them. The rite urges frequent visits to the sick not only by the priest but by the family, friends, and other members of the community of faith. A brief prayer service with the sick, with special prayers for children who are ill, is designed to be led by a priest or by any Christian. The rite for bringing communion to the sick is for use by either the priest or another minister of communion. A shortened rite is also provided for communion in hospitals or institutions.

The liturgy of anointing can be celebrated in several contexts. It may be celebrated for a group of the sick in a communal rite of anointing or for an individual. It may be celebrated within Mass or as a separate rite. It may be celebrated at home, in church, or in a hospital or institution. In all those circumstances the basic elements of the rite are the same.

The introduction to the rite lists three elements as central to the sacrament of the anointing of the sick: the prayer of faith, the laying on of hands, and the anointing with oil (no. 104). It is the prayer of faith that James says will save the sick person. In this sacrament "it is the people of God who pray in faith," the rite notes (no. 105). That is why it is so important that the community of faith gather around the sick person for the celebration of this sacrament. At least family and friends should participate in the sacrament, and ideally some other members of the Church should be part of this little community of faith, representing the whole Church.

The laying on of hands is an ancient gesture that carries several meanings. The touching of the person is itself a source of comfort to one who often feels alone and isolated. It is a gesture Jesus often used to heal the sick. It is a gesture of blessing, symbolizing our prayer for the healing or at least the strengthening of the sick person. And it is a sign of the bestowal of the Holy Spirit, for which we pray. Perhaps because the symbol is so rich and full of meaning, it is done in silence, allowing the symbol itself to speak.

The anointing with oil symbolizes some of the same things as the laying on of hands. Oil has long been used for medicinal purposes, to promote healing and to soothe and comfort the sick. It was also used before athletic contests and in cooking, so oil suggests strength and health. And anointing in the Bible is often a sign of the conferral of the Spirit. In the current rites the sick person is anointed on the forehead while the priest says, "Through this holy anointing, may the Lord in his love and mercy help you with the grace of the Holy Spirit." Then the priest anoints the sick person's hands, saying, "May the Lord who frees you from sin save you and raise you up." According to local custom, other parts of the body may also be anointed, especially the area of pain or injury. The rite recommends an abundant use of the oil so that it will be an effective symbol and notes that the oil should not be wiped off afterwards.

Rites for the Dying

The rites for the pastoral care of the dying center on the celebration of viaticum, either within Mass (which is preferred) or separately. The term "viaticum" is from the Latin *via tecum* which means literally "with you on the way." It refers to the sacrament of the Eucharist for the dying, which is seen as food for the final journey from this life to the next. This celebration of communion is similar to the rite for communion to the sick, with a few additions. The sick person is invited to renew his or her baptismal promises after the homily. After giving communion to the sick person, the minister adds these special words, "May the Lord Jesus Christ protect you and lead you to eternal life." The priest may also give the apostolic pardon, a special plenary indulgence for the dying.

Viaticum is the proper sacrament for the dying. In ordinary circumstances the rite of anointing would have been celebrated much earlier, when the sick person first became seriously ill. It may also have been repeated several times during the illness if the person's condition changed significantly. Viaticum is celebrated when it is clear that the person is dying, but even this celebration should take place while the sick person is still alert and able to participate fully. Viaticum may also be repeated several times if the patient survives for a time.

As death approaches, the sick person is also to be sustained by prayers for the commendation of the dying. This rite includes some short texts and longer readings from Scripture, the litany of the saints, and a prayer of commendation. Special prayers are also provided for the family and for the deceased after death has occurred.

These rites presume long-term pastoral care of the sick by the whole Christian community. It is obvious, of course, that situations will occur in which such long-term care is not possible. For emergency circumstances special rites are provided. One is a continuous rite of penance, anointing, and viaticum, all celebrated on one occasion. If there is not enough time even for this rite, there is a shorter rite for emergencies, in which penance (if desired by the person) is followed immediately by viaticum. Anointing is given later if there is time. That reminds us again that viaticum, not anointing, is the sacrament of the dying, and the Church is concerned to offer that sacrament even if the anointing must be omitted.

"When a priest has been called to attend a person who is already dead," the rite notes "he is not to administer the sacrament of anointing. Instead, he should pray for the dead person, asking that God forgive his or her sins and graciously receive him or her into the kingdom. It is appropriate that he lead the family and friends, if they are present, in some of the prayers suggested at the end of the 'Commendation of the Dying.' . . . If the priest has reason to believe that the person is still living, he may anoint him or her conditionally" (no. 263).

The Meaning of the Sacrament

This overview of the different rites and prayers the Church provides for the care of the sick should give some insight into the meaning of the sacrament of the anointing of the sick. The introduction to the rite describes the effect of the sacrament in terms of the grace of the Spirit by which "the whole person is helped and saved, sustained by trust in God, and strengthened against the temptations of the Evil One and against anxiety over death. Thus the sick person is not only to bear suffering bravely, but also to fight against it. A return to physical health may follow the reception of this sacrament if it will be beneficial to the sick person's salvation. If necessary, the sacrament also provides the sick person with the forgiveness of sins and the completion of Christian penance. In the anointing of the sick, which includes the prayer of faith, faith itself is manifested. . . . The sick person will be saved by personal faith and the faith of the Church, which looks back to the death and resurrection of Christ, the source of the sacrament's power, and looks ahead to the future kingdom that is pledged in the sacraments'' (nos. 6–7).

To understand better the purpose of this sacrament, it can be helpful to reflect a bit on the way that sickness affects a person. One of the first effects of a serious illness is a sense of alienation from one's own body. Instead of being an integral part of the person, the body seems to be rebelling, causing pain and preventing the sick person from functioning normally. This alienation may also be experienced as a loss of control over one's own life. All one's plans and hopes for the future are thrown into question. Life is reduced to the moment, cut off from past activities and from future possibilities.

Such separation from normal activity also brings a sense of alienation from other people. Many times the sick person feels isolated because he or she is prevented from sharing in the activities of family, friends, and work associates. This sense of isolation can be one of the most painful aspects of a serious illness. It may also extend to one's relationship with God. Prayer is often difficult precisely at the time it may be most needed. Faith itself may well be tested, especially if the illness is terminal or long-lasting or very painful.

The Church attempts to respond to those different aspects of the experience of illness by the rites of pastoral care, including the sacraments. Visits with prayer by various members of the community and regular reception of the Eucharist shared with the community help to overcome the sense of isolation and alienation. The sacrament of anointing is the high point of the community's prayer and care for the sick. In this sacrament the community gathers around the sick person, offering support and prayer. The Church seeks to minister to the whole person, praying for healing, offering comfort, strengthening the sick person's faith and hope, and surrounding him or her with the love of Christ. The prayer of the Church supports the prayer of the sick, and the community invites them to unite their sufferings with the redemptive suffering of Christ. Like all the sacraments, the anointing of the sick celebrates the paschal mystery, the death and resurrection of Christ, and invites those who celebrate to enter more fully into that mystery in their own lives. That is the core of the meaning of the sacrament, and it may well be the most important effect of the sacrament.

The sacrament of the anointing of the sick is about healing, but it is a prayer for the healing of the whole person. It may result in physical healing. It may offer healing of the spirit. And since they are interdependent, the sacrament may foster healing of both body and spirit. But the ultimate healing that is desired is a healing of alienation from self, others, and God. Conforming one's life to Christ is what the Christian life is all about. The sacrament of the anointing of the sick fosters that conformation to Christ in the experience of serious illness.

While it is normal that in most cases people will pray for a physical healing, the sacrament does not promise such healing. What it promises is God's help in a time of need. If God judges that bodily healing is best for the sick person, such healing will result from the sacrament. But it may be that God's help will be given as a spiritual strengthening instead. In either case, the sacrament, as a celebration of faith, calls us to accept God's will, to submit in faith to whatever God decides. It invites us to a deeper conformity to Christ, who submitted to the Father's will in his death and resurrection and so came to the fullness of life. This is the ultimate promise of the sacrament—that we, too, will come to fullness of life by uniting ourselves deeply with Christ.

The anointing of the sick requires a priest or bishop for its celebration, according to the current discipline of the Church. Much discussion has occurred recently about the possibility of extending this ministry to others, especially deacons, who are often deeply involved in the pastoral care of the sick. Since history indicates that even lay people could anoint the sick in the early Church, it is possible that we will see such an extension in the years ahead. Even with the anointing restricted, it is clear that the broader pastoral care of the sick is the responsibility of the whole Christian community.

At this point a word might be said about the charismatic prayer for healing that is popular among many today. Such prayer has obvious connections to the sacramental ministry, but it should also be distinguished from it. Both are prayers of faith, and both manifest the community's concern for the sick person. The charismatic healing service seeks miraculous healings, though it does generally recognize that God may heal the person in other ways beyond physical healing. The sacramental ministry is focused more on union with the paschal mystery of Christ, whether or not the sacrament brings about a cure. While the Church recognizes and welcomes the charismatic healing ministry, the sacrament of the anointing of the sick is the official and central way in which the Church ministers to the sick.

Practical Pointers

A proper understanding of the anointing of the sick can guide us to proper decisions about the sacrament. One of the most basic decisions is when to celebrate the anointing. The introduction to the rite itself gives guidelines for this decision. "Great care and concern should be taken," it says, "to see that those of the faithful whose health is seriously impaired by sickness or old age receive this sacrament" (no. 8). A footnote on this sentence adds: "The word *periculose* has been carefully studied and rendered as 'seriously,' rather than as 'gravely,' 'dangerously,' or 'perilously.' Such a rendering will serve to avoid restrictions upon the celebration of the sacrament. On the one hand, the sacrament may and should be given to anyone whose health is seriously impaired; on the other hand, it may not be given indiscriminately or to any person whose health is not seriously impaired."

Those words indicate the kind of judgment that should be made. The proper recipient of this sacrament is someone who is seriously ill; the patient need not be near death, nor should a person be anointed for a clearly minor illness. As the introduction concludes, a "prudent or reasonably sure judgment, without scruple, is sufficient for deciding on the seriousness of an illness" (no. 8). The sacrament may also be repeated if the person recovers and then falls ill again or if the patient's illness becomes more serious.

It has become common for the sick to be anointed before surgery. The rite approves of that whenever a serious illness is the reason for the surgery. The elderly may be anointed if they have become weakened by age, even though no serious illness is present, since their health is impaired simply by the advancing years.

Children may also be anointed "if they have sufficient use of reason to be strengthened by this sacrament" (no. 12). Here again a reasonable judgment is sufficient. A child may find comfort in the sacrament even if the ability to express an understanding of the rites is lacking. The sacramental imposition of hands and anointing with oil can be a comforting touch of the Lord, and the prayer of faith may be consoling even to a young child. If a child is dying, the rites also recommend that the sacraments of initiation (baptism, confirmation, and Eucharist) be celebrated, even if the child is younger than the usual age for those sacraments (nos. 172-73).

There has been considerable discussion and confusion about the use of this sacrament in cases of mental illness. The question is addressed in the introduction to the rite, which says that "those who are judged to have a serious mental illness and who would be strengthened by the sacrament may be anointed" (no. 53). It would be advisable in such cases to consult with the sick person's doctor to determine if the anointing would likely be a help and consolation to the patient.

It is important to remember that this sacrament finds its proper place in the context of a broad-ranging pastoral care of the sick by the whole Christian community. With the anointing of the sick, as with all the sacraments, any magical notions should be avoided. Sacraments are human experiences, and their benefits depend in large measure on the way we prepare for and celebrate them. Certainly God will bless and care for the sick even if we do a poor job of pastoral care. But attentive and loving care of the sick and careful and reverent celebration of the sacraments can support and deepen the effect of God's action in the sacrament. Sacraments are meant to be high points in our experience of God's presence in our lives; good pastoral care of the sick by all members of the Christian community can make that presence evident to the sick throughout their illness.

The sacrament itself should be celebrated in a communal setting whenever possible. In some cases a communal celebration at which several sick people are anointed together can be arranged. But even when only one person is to be anointed, the Christian community should gather for the celebration. Ideally the gathering should include a number of fellow parishioners of the sick person. If that is not possible, at least members of the family should be present to join in the celebration. In contrast to past practice, when the family often left the room while the sacrament was celebrated (perhaps because penance was usually included in the rites), the current rites presume the presence of family, friends, and other members of the Church whenever possible. This is a gathering in faith around an ailing brother or sister, and "this prayer uttered in faith will reclaim the one who is ill" (Jas 5:15).

A final practical reminder is that the proper sacrament of the dying is viaticum, the reception of communion as food for the journey to heaven. It is meant to be a consolation for the patient, so it should be celebrated while the sick person can actively participate. If possible, the celebration of the Mass is to be preferred as the context for viaticum. That can often be arranged as a small-group Mass in the hospital or nursing home or at home. If a Mass cannot be arranged, the celebration of viaticum should still be a communal rite, celebrated with a gathering of Christians around the dying person.

Conclusion

The experience of serious illness is always a time of trial for the patient and for friends and relatives. Illness brings us face to face with our mortality and disrupts many aspects of our normal lives and relationships. The needs of the sick are great, going far beyond physical and medical needs. The Christian community tries to respond to those needs generously, imitating the love and care of Christ himself for the sick in body and spirit. The revised rites for the pastoral care of the sick and the dying offer a rich resource for the Church community. May the Holy Spirit strengthen all members of the Church to manifest the love of Christ clearly to the sick in their midst.

DISCUSSION/REFLECTION QUESTIONS

1. Have you come to understand the sacrament of anointing as truly a sacrament of the sick and not just of the dying? If so, what helped you to make that shift?

2. What changed in the shifting view of this sacrament in the ninth century? What was lost? What was gained?

3. What do the current rites take from the first eight centuries, and what do they incorporate from the later history?

4. Have you ever been part of the celebration of anointing of the sick? Was it in a communal celebration or an individual one? What impressed you most about the celebration?

5. When should the anointing of the sick be celebrated? Can you think of some situations in your own life or the life of someone you know when the sacrament would have been appropriate and helpful?

6. How do you decide when someone is "seriously ill," and who should make that judgment?

7. Why is viaticum the proper sacrament for the dying?

8. What is the purpose of the sacrament of the anointing of the sick? How does it fit into the larger ministry to the sick that the Church encourages?

9. Do you think that this sacrament would be helpful for a young child? How young? How would you decide if a child understands enough to celebrate this sacrament with him or her?

10. How important is the presence of a community of the faithful in the celebration of the anointing of the sick? Why?

Sacraments of Vocation

Chapter 6

MARRIAGE
Symbol of God's Love

It's not recorded in the Book of Genesis, but rumor has it that as Adam and Eve were being expelled from the Garden of Eden, the first man turned to his mate and commented, "You know, honey, it's tough living in an age of transition!" The rumor reminds us that every age is an age of transition and that married couples face many changes in their life together, no matter who they are. Yet it can be argued that no previous era has thrown so many elements of change into the cauldron at one time. The pace of change has increased dramatically in this century, and numerous social forces have been exerting pressure on the institution of marriage.

Couples who enter marriage today do not have the clearly defined roles of earlier generations. The women's liberation movement has significantly altered the way both men and women understand their respective roles in society and in the marriage relationship. Moreover, since liberation involves a gradual raising of consciousness, many relationships shift drastically after the marriage commitment has been made. It takes a great deal of maturity and a lot of communication to maintain a healthy marriage through such transitions.

Married couples also face more transitions today than in past ages simply because of a dramatically improved life expectancy, which makes the commitment to a lifetime relationship longer than it used to be. A longer life expectancy is certainly a good thing, but it does require that married couples learn how to change and grow together through many stages of life and changes in lifestyle and circumstances.

Recent decades have also seen a revolution in sexual mores, affecting couples both in their own relationship and in their relationships with others. A general rejection of previous social restraints on sexual activity outside of marriage makes faithfulness more difficult to maintain. Perhaps more important is the stress given in our culture to sexual attractiveness and performance as central in any romantic relationship. While sex is obviously important in a marriage, putting it center stage can short-circuit the development of other aspects of a healthy relationship of love.

Something of a counterbalance to the emphasis on sex is an increasing stress on communication and meeting one another's emotional needs. Communication is rightly seen as essential to maintaining a healthy relationship. The stress on meeting each other's needs, however, is often unrealistic. Each of us needs a variety of people to care for us and support us. Our culture has developed a high degree of mobility, with people pulling up roots and moving to another part of the country (or another country) perhaps several times in their lives. The result is frequently a distancing from relatives and old friends. The loss of the extended family relationships and the difficulty of forming lasting friendships in a highly mobile lifestyle lead many couples to look solely to each other for support. Too often that asks more than one relationship can bear, and the marriage self-destructs.

This cursory look at contemporary social forces affecting marriage can give us some understanding of the high divorce rate in our culture. There are many other factors involved as well, including the divorce rate itself. Since divorce has become so common, it has also become more acceptable. In contrast to earlier eras, when society urged couples to stay together and often sustained them through difficult periods, social pressure today often urges couples to divorce if they find themselves unhappy for even a short time.

Marriage as Sacrament

Understanding the social forces affecting marriage is important because marriage is fundamentally a social reality. Yet Christians have long seen marriage as a sacrament too, which is to say that they have seen it as capable of revealing something of the mystery of God. That insight began with the Hebrew prophets, long before the Christian era. Hosea saw God's faithfulness to Israel reflected in his own experience of faithfulness to his wife, Gomer, despite her repeated unfaithfulness. As Yahweh never gave up on Israel, Hosea felt called to continually forgive his errant spouse. Prophets after him kept alive the tradition of seeing the relationship of God and the people in terms of marriage.

In the New Testament the teaching of Jesus on marriage centers almost exclusively on his rejection of divorce, in contrast to many of the rabbis of his time, who permitted divorce for a variety of reasons. St. Paul continues the prophetic tradition of seeing marriage as reflecting the love of God, casting the image in terms of Christ and the Church (see Ephesians 5), which he calls a "great mystery."

The Greek term Paul used, *mysterion*, was translated into Latin as *sacramentum*, and thus marriage began to be called a sacrament. It is important to note, however, that this was a broad sense of sacrament, not the carefully defined notion of later centuries. It was not until the eleventh and twelfth centuries that theologians agreed that there are seven sacraments in the limited sense, and marriage was the last to be added to the list. The early Church saw many things as revealing God's love and activity, and those were termed sacramental in the broad sense.

Though the early Christians saw the religious dimension of marriage (everything had a religious significance in Christ), they did not celebrate marriage in church or as a liturgical service. Marriage was celebrated according to the social customs of the time, but Christians recognized that their marriages, like every part of their lives, were to be transformed by grace and lived "in the Lord." Marriage was not sacramental because it was begun in church but because it reflected the love of Christ for the Church. And as Christ is always faithful, so marriage was seen to be an unbreakable commitment.

Beginning in the fourth century, Christians began to celebrate a service of prayer and blessing after the legal marriage. That was not a church marriage, nor was it required for all Christians. Soon the lower orders of the clergy (e.g., lectors, porters, acolytes) were required to have their marriages blessed after the legal ceremony, though that was not required for the laity. For centuries the actual form of the marriage varied according to local customs and traditions.

Gradually, from the ninth to the eleventh century, the juridical control of marriage itself passed from the state to the Church, and marriage began to be celebrated in the context of a church liturgy. In the eleventh and twelfth centuries theologians struggled to develop a theology of sacraments and to determine which church celebrations were sacraments in the strict sense. Marriage was included in the list of seven, probably because there was such a long tradition of calling marriage a sacrament. Yet it was not until later centuries that marriage was accorded full sacramental status, even though it was listed among the seven, since the medieval theologians had difficulty seeing marriage as a source of grace. That was due partly to a negative view of sexuality that has plagued the Church for centuries and partly to the fact that marriage obviously preceded Christ, while the other sacraments were seen as stemming from Christ.

The Council of Trent in the sixteenth century defended marriage as a sacrament in the strict sense against some of the Reformers who rejected its sacramentality. Largely in an attempt to regulate secret marriages, this same Council also required Catholics to be married before a priest and two witnesses. That requirement has been in force since that time, though exceptions are made when a priest is not available (as in some mission situations) and when there is sufficient reason for the marriage to be celebrated in another Christian Church or a different religion or even in a civil ceremony.

The twentieth century has seen some significant developments of the theology of marriage. The Code of Canon Law, issued in 1917, for example, saw marriage primarily in terms of a contract between the two parties. The Second Vatican Council and the revision of the Code of Canon Law, issued in 1983, see marriage more as a covenant between the spouses, reflecting the covenant between God and humanity.

That shift has numerous consequences. A contract is a legal reality that confers certain rights and imposes certain responsibilities. Both parties to the contract must be of legal age and are bound to fulfill the terms of the contract. Contracts can be made between friends, but in itself a contract is a very impersonal agreement. A covenant, on the other hand, is a bond of love between the parties and is intensely personal. Like a contract, it also involves certain rights and responsibilities, but it goes far beyond a contract, since it includes a personal commitment of both parties to the welfare of the other.

While a contract is clearly limited in its scope, a covenant establishes a relationship that cannot be so easily defined. The covenant relationship is open-ended. It is the relationship itself that is central, not the specified rights and duties, and the growth and development of the relationship may make demands that were not even envisioned at the beginning. That is a much more personal image, and the Council put more emphasis on the personal relationship between the couple than earlier ages did. That is beginning to affect the way the whole Church understands marriage and is the basis for much of the theology of marriage that is being developed in our own time.

Secular Reality—Saving Mystery

This all too brief survey of the history of Christian marriage indicates the difficulty the Church has had in trying to define marriage as a sacrament. It also reveals, however, that Christians have consistently seen the social or secular reality of marriage as a revelation of God's love. The love of husband and wife is a powerful and effective symbol of God's love for us. If we understand God's saving work primarily as a process of reconciliation, of reuniting human beings with God and with one another, then it is easy to see marriage as a rich symbol of God's work. Christ himself has been described as the marriage of humanity and divinity in his incarnation. The marriage union reflects that union which is fundamental to our salvation. That has prompted at least one theologian to see marriage as the premier sacrament, the premier symbol of God's saving activity.

In calling marriage a sacrament, Christians sometimes refer to the wedding celebration. But often the term "sacrament" is used in a broader sense to refer to the state of marriage itself. The living out of the marriage relationship itself can reveal God's presence and love. This perspective sees marriage more as covenant than as contract. It is not just a legal bond conferring certain rights and duties, but a deep bond of love and commitment, modeled on the covenant between Christ and the Church. The marriage covenant can be a means of grace for the spouses. Each of us must learn to be open to God's love in order to accept the gift of grace and salvation. For many people, it is marriage that teaches them to be open. In the constant and forgiving love of a spouse, they come to trust in the possibility of love and the goodness of reality. That, in turn, enables them to believe in the love of God for them and the goodness of creation and creation's Lord. While many people, of course, first learn those truths from loving parents, the experience of marital love and fidelity remains for many a powerful teacher on a more mature level.

Those who enter into Christian marriage should learn to see the love of God for them precisely in the love of their spouse. God loves each of them in a very powerful way through their spouse; the love of husband or wife is one of the deepest experiences of love, and all true love is a sharing in the love of God. Many writers, including the Fathers of the Second Vatican Council, have spoken of the Christian family as a domestic church, a place where the love of God and religious faith are learned and celebrated. Married love is not quite the same as the *agape* of the New Testament, which is a totally self-sacrificing love, since married love seeks mutuality and requires a certain exclusiveness. Nevertheless, married love certainly teaches self-sacrificing love and leads the partners to become more loving persons. It is therefore an important school for love and for conversion to the Christian lifestyle of loving service.

If family life is to achieve its potential as a domestic church, married couples must learn to share their faith deeply. Many couples have found that sharing prayer together is a powerful way to deepen both their faith and their mutual love. To share openly with a spouse one's personal relationship to God is to open oneself deeply to the other. That is always a risk, but at the same time it enables the couple to draw on the power of God in their life together. No Christian community, large or small, can be faithful to the gospel without constant prayer. Shared prayer helps the couple, precisely as couple, to be closely united to the Lord, and it also forms a good basis for introducing children to the life of faith and prayer.

All of us, of course, know of marriages in which that picture has not been realized, of marriages that do not last and marriages that last only as a shared misery. Even the best marriages have a hard time measuring up to the exalted ideals of theology. That does not necessarily mean that the theology is unrealistic. Sacraments are human symbols and therefore always incomplete. We never fully achieve the ideals, yet keeping the goal in mind is essential to keep us striving toward it.

It is also important to recognize that a successful marriage is not a purely human accomplishment. The love that sustains a lifetime commitment is possible only through the power of Christ, through the power of God's love at work in the spouses' love for each other. It is also important for Christians to remember that the cross is an integral part of Christian life. The depth of Christ's love is expressed in the total gift of himself on the cross; the depth of married love will also find expression in the self-sacrificing love of a spouse in times of suffering and difficulty.

Saint Paul said that the relationship between marriage and Christ's love is a great mystery. Both sides of the mystery illuminate each other. The experience of marriage helps us to understand the love of Christ for us. At the same time the love of Christ, expressed in his life, death, and resurrection, helps us to understand the marriage commitment and the necessity of embracing suffering in marriage in order to achieve the depth of love that Christ makes possible.

Marriage as a Vocation in the Church

Seen in the light of God's continuing work of redemption, marriage is easily understood as a vocation in the Church. Each

Christian is called to live out his or her baptism in a particular vocation. For some it is a vocation of full-time work for the Church; for others it is a vocation to the single life in the world; but for the majority of the baptized, marriage is the vocation within which they will live out their baptismal commitment.

We noted earlier the concentration in our time on the personal relationship between the couple. While much of that is positive, there is also a danger of forgetting the social dimensions of marriage and the importance of the marriage relationship to society as a whole. In a similar way, there is a danger for Christians of seeing marriage too exclusively in terms of the couple themselves and neglecting the importance of marriage as a vocation, as a way of being Christian, as a role of service within the Church. All Christians are called to their vocations to be of service to others. Those who are married and those who are preparing for marriage need to reflect deeply on their role within the Church community. In their marriage, Christian spouses are called to witness constantly to God's love by loving each other and by sharing their love with others. Taking on this vocation means accepting the responsibility for carrying on the work of the Church, and doing so specifically as a married couple. The marriage of Christians, therefore, is always of great importance to the whole Christian community. For the couple themselves, marriage should be the primary way they grow in faith and in their relationship with God.

The Necessity of Faith

When we understand Christian marriage as a vocation and as a sacrament, it becomes obvious that taking on this vocation requires faith and a commitment to Church membership. That presents a serious difficulty today, for many couples want to be married at a time when they are going through what has become a common crisis of faith, including rejection of the institutional Church. Many young people in our culture leave the Church sometime after high school, often returning a few years later after coming to a personal decision of faith. Unfortunately many want to be married before they have worked out their relationship with the Church and so find it difficult, if not impossible, to honestly accept the responsibilities of marriage as a sacrament and a vocation in the Church.

In many cases pastors find it necessary to delay the marriage in order to allow time to work with the couple and try to resolve the questions of faith and Church membership. There are other reasons why marriages are delayed, but the question of faith is one that causes much anguish and misunderstanding. There is much discussion today on how the Church can deal with the problem.

One very interesting experiment was begun in the diocese of Autun, France, in the 1970s. Facing a large percentage of the population that was baptized but not active in the Church, the bishop there has established three options for the marriage of Christians. The first is civil marriage, conducted at the city hall and recognized by the Church as valid but not as a sacrament. The second is called "marriage with welcome"; following a civil marriage, the couple celebrates a religious ritual of readings and prayer with friends and relatives and the priest, in church or at home. The third option, for those who have a deeper faith and Christian commitment, is sacramental marriage celebrated in the midst of the Church community.

Those options correspond to different levels of faith: those with little or no faith celebrate marriage as a civil matter; those with some faith in God but with no real relationship to the Church celebrate a civil marriage followed by a religious service; those who are committed to Christ and the Church celebrate marriage as a sacrament. Couples in the first two groups may come to deeper faith later in life and may wish to celebrate marriage as a sacrament at that time.

While those options are just an experiment and go beyond the provisions of current canon law, the experiment has been conducted in consultation with the Vatican and has also been adopted by a number of other dioceses. It gives us an indication of one possible direction for the Church in the future. Another possibility suggested by some authors involves a much more intensive preparation for marriage. Perhaps modeled on the Rite of Christian Initiation of Adults, such a process would involve both extended reflection and interaction with the Christian community on the meaning of marriage and periodic celebrations of rites marking the engagement and other stages in the movement of a couple toward readiness to celebrate the sacrament.

Preparation for Marriage

Many dioceses have begun to move in the direction of more extensive and intensive preparation for marriage. It is common today for a diocese to require that the parish be notified six months before the wedding so that there will be adequate time for preparation. The preparation often includes some form of written questionnaire about the couple's values and beliefs and expectations. It also frequently involves extended discussions with the priest and/or a married couple about the realities of married life, focusing especially on any problems of the couple that surface. Sometimes the preparation also includes a Pre-Cana course or an Engaged Encounter weekend or some other organized pre-marriage program. Finally, the couple plan the marriage celebration, working with the priest and other liturgical ministers.

The purpose of such extensive preparation is twofold. First, it is intended to determine the readiness of the couple to undertake the responsibilities of Christian marriage. The priest who witnesses the marriage must be confident that the couple are adequately prepared and that the marriage can be expected to last and to be an effective symbol of Christ's love. To preside at a wedding without such assurance is to celebrate the sacrament dishonestly, proclaiming to the Church and to the world what is not true. Some dioceses do not allow setting the date for the wedding until the presiding priest or deacon is confident of the couple's readiness.

The second purpose of preparation is related to the first, namely, to give the couple as much help as possible toward a successful and happy marriage. The high divorce rate today, even among Catholics, reminds us of the importance of adequate preparation. Many secular commentators have noted the strange fact that we educate and train people before they enter a career or start working on a job, we teach them how to drive before they get a license, we coach them in sports before they play in a game, yet our society provides almost no training or education for marriage or parenthood. Even in the Church we insist on years of training before a man is ordained as a priest or deacon, but we are content with a few hours of preparation before marriage. The assumption is that everyone knows how to handle the basic responsibilities of married life, but the current divorce rate and the frequency of domestic violence and child abuse should make us question that assumption.

Of course, the preparation needed for marriage and parenting cannot be accomplished in six months or even a year before the wedding. What is needed is a lifetime training in the meaning of Christian marriage. Children need to be taught by their parents from their early years that marriage for Christians is a sacrament and a vocation. Then there will be a basis upon which marriage ministers can build when it comes time for the immediate preparation. It is also important that Christian communities find better ways to support newly married couples in their life together. Recognizing that most marriages that fail do so because of problems that arise in the first few years of marriage, more and more dioceses are trying to offer support to the newly married through support groups, discussion programs, and sponsor couples.

Celebrating the Sacrament

We have spoken of marriage as a sacrament in the broad sense as a state of life. In the strict sense, the sacrament is the celebration of the marriage by the Christian community surrounding the couple. The sacramental celebration is the way the community celebrates the love of God that it recognizes in the love between this man and this woman. The sacrament celebrates their love and their commitment to each other and at the same time reinforces that love and commitment by proclaiming it to the whole community. The wedding really functions as a rite of passage into the married state. What is proclaimed and celebrated at the wedding is to be lived out over a whole lifetime. It is for this reason that we can use the term "sacrament" for the married state as well as for the wedding itself.

Understanding the wedding as a celebration of the whole Church around the couple provides the basis for proper planning of the event. The first principle in planning is to remember that Christian marriage, like every sacrament, is celebrated by the whole community. The couple are the ministers of the sacrament to each other and thus are at the center of the celebration. But they are also to minister to the whole assembly, and proper wedding planning will ensure that the whole assembly participates fully in the liturgical action.

Some radical rethinking on the part of many couples and many families is needed. Weddings are more often style shows and exercises in superstition than liturgical celebrations of prayer and worship. That may sound like a harsh judgment, but it is simply a description of what occurs at many weddings. Much more attention is paid to what the bride and bridesmaids are wearing than to the liturgy itself. All too often even faithful Church members sit through a wedding as if they have forgotten all the responses and songs, participating like spectators at a show rather than like members of a worshiping community. And much concern is shown for such superstitions as starting the wedding on the half-hour (for good luck), not allowing the groom to see the bride before the wedding, and throwing rice on the couple (an old pagan fertility symbol), none of which can claim a proper place in Christian liturgy.

Some couples have begun to create new wedding traditions that are more in keeping with the idea of weddings as sacramental celebrations and times of worship. The bride and groom, for example, greet the members of the assembly as they arrive at church, expressing their joy at having them present for the celebration and encouraging them to participate fully. That is an appropriate gesture, since the couple are, in a sense, the hosts of the celebration and have invited the assembly to join in the celebration of their love.

It is becoming common today to have the bridesmaids and groomsmen process down the aisle together and to have the groom's parents accompany him and the bride's parents accompany her down the aisle. That is more appropriate than the ''style show'' entrance and suggests that this is the beginning of a service of worship. That is suggested even more clearly if the music for the procession is a congregational hymn, since that is the way we usually begin our worship together. These and other creative decisions can do much to help the whole congregation realize that the wedding is a time for prayer and worship, not a time to sit back as spectators.

An area of special concern in wedding planning is the question of music. Often the couple has special songs, usually from the current pop charts, which they want played at the wedding because those songs are important to the two of them. While that desire is understandable, it leads to choices of music that are often inappropriate. The Christian wedding is a time of worship and prayer, and the music used should be an expression of Christian faith and should be conducive to the prayer of the whole assembly. It should include pieces that can be sung by the assembly so that they can participate fully in the celebration. There is room for some solo pieces or choir music, but the assembly should not be excluded from its proper participation. A brief rehearsal with the congregation before the service begins would help them to participate well.

The participation of the assembly is important because the sacramental celebration is their celebration too. It will have an effect on them, reaffirming their own commitment to love in their own lives (married or single), as well as affirming the commitment of the newly married couple. That is part of the ministry that the newly married offer to the larger Church.

The Issue of Indissolubility

Up to this point we have skirted the contemporary questions about the indissolubility of marriage. That was intentional, because that issue so often dominates discussions of Christian marriage, overshadowing the great richness of the Christian tradition on marriage. While debate on how the Church should respond to those whose marriages have failed is important, it is even more important that the whole Christian community recover a vital sense of what Christian marriage can and should be.

When we examine the tradition of the Church from the very beginning, we find that the permanence of the commitment has always been a deep concern of the Church community. The words of Jesus on divorce are strong ones, and the Church has always tried to live up to that demanding vision. For the first thousand years or so, Church teaching stressed that divorce and remarriage were not *permitted* in light of the moral demands of Jesus. Later theologians taught that divorce and remarriage were not even *possible*, because the marriage bond continued to exist even if the couple separated. Only death could end a valid, sacramental, and consummated marriage.

Along with its deep concern to preserve the indissolubility of marriage, the Church has always tried to offer support and compassion to those whose marriages have failed. Feeling bound by the words of Christ, the Church has not been able to approve of new marriages for all those who have experienced divorce, but it has tried to do whatever it felt was possible. The whole system of marriage tribunals is designed to try to balance these two pastoral concerns of preserving the indissolubility of marriages and still helping those who find themselves in difficult situations.

The marriage tribunal seeks simply to determine whether a given marriage was in fact a valid, sacramental, and consummated marriage. If it can be shown that the marriage was not valid, the tribunal declares the marriage null and void, and thus the parties are free to marry. Since many divorces occur because of problems that were inherent in the marriage from the very beginning, many of the unions were not true marriages; an annulment establishes the absence of the lifelong bond, and the parties are considered never to have been married. In certain other cases where the marriage was valid but not consummated or not sacramental, the Church feels it can dissolve the marriage.

A tribunal solution, of course, is not open to all divorced couples, since some divorces occur even though the marriage was valid and consummated and sacramental. In those cases the tribunal cannot declare the marriage null and void, so the parties are not free to enter another marriage. The Church then tries to offer understanding and support as it counsels the parties to live a single lifestyle as long as their spouse is still living. Even when such a person remarries civilly without Church approval, the Church today seeks to be as understanding and helpful as possible. Since it cannot accept the new union as a marriage, the Church insists that those people are excluded from receiving communion as long as they remain in the invalid relationship, but even then she urges them to come to church, to remain as active as they can, and to stay close to the Lord.

Unfortunately the Church's efforts to encourage permanence and to discourage divorce have often led to a very negative attitude toward those who have experienced a divorce. That has caused many of the divorced and separated to feel rejected by the Church community, precisely at a time when they need the support of the community the most. Such an attitude is especially inappropriate when people have been divorced but have not remarried and are trying to be faithful to their original commitment despite separation from their spouses. Such Catholics are in full communion with the Church and should be fully accepted and supported by their fellow Catholics. Even when a person has chosen to remarry without Church recognition, the Church community should try to reflect the mercy of God and not judge harshly. Only God can know the full circumstances of a person's life and decisions, and only God has a right to judge.

The history of the Church reveals some variation in the way the Church has handled situations of divorce. Those variations and exceptions, combined with recognition of the increasing number of people who have experienced divorce and want somehow to remarry in the Church, have led contemporary theologians to discuss possible changes in Church law and practice. Some of the debate revolves around just what is necessary for a marriage to be truly sacramental (currently the Church considers every marriage between two baptized people, even non-Catholics, to be a sacrament). Discussion also revolves around the question of whether it is possible in any way for the Church to allow remarriage after divorce in some cases. It is impossible at this point to forecast the outcome of those theological discussions, but it is unlikely that there will be a resolution of those issues in the near future. The problems are complex and take a long time to resolve. Whatever the outcome of the debate, however, it is certain that the Church will always strive to keep the ideal of permanent commitment strong and clear. Marriage should be forever—that is clear from psychology and the experience of the married as well as from the words of Christ. However the Church decides to deal with those situations in which the ideal has not been achieved, we must do everything possible to help couples enter into and sustain relationships of such depth of love and self-sacrifice that they will be true reflections of God's love.

Conclusion

Though it was the last sacrament added to the official list, marriage is vital for the Church's life and mission. It is the most common way that Christians live out their baptismal vocation and the first and most basic school of Christian life and belief for children. It is crucial, then, that the whole Christian assembly strive together to recover the richness of our traditional vision of what Christian marriage can and should be.

The vision alone is not enough, of course. It will take much work to make that vision become reality in the lives of those who are married and those who are preparing to enter marriage. The work is really more the responsibility of the married than of the professional clergy. That vision of marriage must be taught in the home and exemplified by married couples if it is to grasp the imagination and the hearts of the community. Words and formal teaching (like this book) are important, but example is still the best teacher. May the Lord give to all married Christians the courage and depth of love necessary to be faithful to their commitment and to be effective sacraments of God's love for all people.

DISCUSSION/REFLECTION QUESTIONS

1. What do you think are the most serious challenges to marriage in our time? What can the Christian community do to help couples meet those challenges?

2. Why is marriage called a sacrament in the Christian tradition? Why did it take so long for it to be officially included among the sacraments?

3. Do you understand the difference between a contract and a covenant? What difference does it make in your marriage or your understanding of marriage?

4. When you think of marriage as a sacrament, do you think primarily of the wedding or of the living out of the marriage relationship? Why?

5. Is the Christian ideal of marriage unrealistic, or can it work in practice? Why do you think so many Christian marriages end in divorce today? What can be done to decrease the divorce rate?

6. If you are married, have you been aware of the love of God at work in your marriage? If you are not married, can you think of couples in whom that love is evident to you?

7. How can the Church help people understand marriage as a true vocation in the Church community?

8. How important is faith in your own marriage? In the marriages of people you know?

9. What do you think the Church should do when couples ask to be married but have no active faith or commitment to the Church? Does the Autun experiment make sense to you? Are there better solutions?

10. What kind of preparation for marriage is required or provided in your parish? How could it be improved?

11. In your experience of weddings, have they really been prayerful celebrations of the Church's liturgy? What hinders that kind of celebration and what fosters it?

12. Do you understand the Church's teaching on the indissolubility of marriage? Do you agree with the Church's traditional interpretation of Christ's command? Why or why not?

Chapter 7

HOLY ORDERS
Sacrament of Service

In the summer of 1985 the Archdiocese of Cincinnati released a report projecting the number of priests in active ministry that the archdiocese can expect in the last part of the twentieth century. The study, conducted by Fr. Robert Thorsen, was appropriately entitled "A Plunge to Scarcity," for it forecast a steep decline in the number of priests available to serve the 260 parishes of the archdiocese. From a current total of 339 priests, the sociological data indicates that the archdiocese will have between 190 and 230 priests in the year 2000. In response, the archdiocese has initiated a program called "For the Harvest" to develop grass-roots planning in every parish to ensure high-quality parish ministry in the years ahead with a smaller number of priests.

What is striking about such projections is that they are in no way unique to the Cincinnati Archdiocese. The same type of precipitous decline is occurring throughout the country, as well as around the world. The effects of this "plunge to scarcity" are beginning to be felt in many dioceses, and Church officials are scrambling to develop plans to cope with the situation.

A Priest Shortage?

In light of our recent past, the situation is often termed a "priest shortage" or a "vocation crisis." While it is clear that the number of priests is declining, a broader look at Church history suggests other ways of understanding this change and offers hope of renewed vitality in the Church's ministry. Such hope depends, however, on the willingness of Church members to look beyond their personal histories and accept the directions in which the Spirit of God may be leading us.

The sacrament of holy orders may very well be the least understood of the seven rituals we call sacraments. It is the sacrament celebrated the least often in the Church, and celebrated around the smallest number of people. Most Catholics have never been part of the celebration of holy orders. Moreover, it is a pluriform sacrament, embracing the ordination of deacons, priests (presbyters), and bishops. And it has changed since most of us were young, for it used to include the subdiaconate and four minor orders as well (porter, lector, exorcist, and acolyte).

Entering an Order

The most fundamental misunderstanding involves the meaning of ordination itself. For a long time we have looked at ordination primarily as the conferral of special powers upon the ordained individual. Like all misunderstanding, there is some truth in that approach, but it misses the fundamental meaning of holy orders.

Good sacramental theology always begins by studying the actual celebration of the sacraments, and the rites of ordination themselves indicate the basic meaning of holy orders. In the ordination of a bishop, the new bishop is consecrated by at least three other bishops, but "it is fitting for all the bishops present together with the principal consecrator to ordain the bishop-elect" (no. 2 of the introduction to the rite). All the bishops present lay hands on the head of the new bishop during the celebration. In a similar way, all the priests present at the ordination of a new priest (presbyter) impose hands on the new member of their order. In the ordination of a deacon, all the deacons present are invited to give the new deacon the sign of peace right after the bishop, thus welcoming him into their order.

In each of those rites it is clear that those being ordained are entering an order. One does not "receive" an order; one "enters" an order, a concrete group of people who are chosen and recognized by the Church for a particular ministry. As the bishop-elect is told, "never forget that . . . you are incorporated into the college of bishops" (no. 18). Ordination is not so much a conferral of personal powers upon an individual as it is initiation into an order of ministry established by the Church for service to the Christian community.

A Look at History

A brief look at the history of ministry in the Church can be very enlightening, especially to those who assume that the current shape of Church structure is as old as the Church itself. The shape of the Church's ministerial orders has been much more varied than most of us have imagined.

The New Testament period

The New Testament shows us a Church with a variety of structures and ministries. Jesus did not establish bishops, priests (presbyters), and deacons. The only ministerial structure he established, the Twelve, was not maintained long. Matthias was chosen to replace Judas, but after that the Twelve were not replaced when they died.

Different local Churches developed varied forms of leadership. Though the evidence is limited, the Churches founded by Paul seem to have developed a charismatic structure, based on gifts of the Spirit manifested in various individuals and groups. He lists apostles, prophets, evangelists, pastors, teachers, miracle- workers, healers, assistants, administrators, and those who speak in tongues (see 1 Cor 12:28 and Eph 4:11), among others. Other Churches adopted a structure that was common in the Jewish synagogue, with a council of elders (presbyters) directing the Church's life. In some of them there was a head of the council, called the overseer (*episkopos*) or bishop. Eventually the bishop-presbyter model came to prevail, but there was great variety in those early years. Late in the New Testament period we also see the development of the order of deacons, who were assistants to the bishop.

The post-New Testament era

Among the various charismatic ministries, prophets and teachers seem to have been especially important (see 1 Cor 12:28), and another early Church document gives us a valuable insight into their role. The *Didache*, written in the early second century, around the same time as the later New Testament books, indicates that prophets and teachers had customarily presided at the Eucharist. The *Didache* seems to be encouraging the communities to which it was addressed to choose bishops and deacons to replace the prophets and teachers, since they performed the same service to the Church. What is happening here is a shift from wandering and charismatic ministries to a more stable and structured ministry. The office of prophet and teacher was eventually absorbed into the role of bishop, and the bishop increasingly appears as the dominant figure, gradually standing out from the council of elders (presbyters) as a separate order and the chief minister of the Church.

It is important to note here that presiding at the Eucharist was not restricted to bishops and priests (presbyters). What seems to have been the operative principle was that whoever was recognized as the community's leader was accepted as the presider at Eucharist, whether that was an apostle, a prophet, a teacher, or a bishop. That principle was very strong in the early Church, so much so that the Council of Chalcedon (451) forbade the ordination of anyone unless a local community was assigned to him. Those ordained had to be the leaders of local communities. Ordination was not a personal possession but the recognition and affirmation of a leadership role in the Church community. That principle about ordination reminds us that the early Church saw no separation between its worship and its daily life. Worship was the expression of the Church's life, and so the leader of the community was the leader of worship.

From presbyter to priest

It is also interesting to note that the New Testament and the post-New Testament Church did not speak of the presider in priestly terms. The Letter to the Hebrews is very clear that Jesus is the only priest in the New Covenant, in contrast to the multiple priesthood of the Old Testament. In its concern to make clear the difference between the two covenants, the early Church avoided using priestly language in reference to its ministers. At the same time, the New Testament itself sees the Eucharist as linked to the sacrifice of Jesus, and sacrifice is a priestly action, so it was inevitable that the bishop would eventually begin to be seen as a priest. Once the Church had clearly distanced itself from Judaism and Old Testament worship, that is precisely what happened. The bishop was seen more and more as the new high priest presiding over the Eucharistic celebration of Christ's sacrifice.

At first, of course, that applied only to the bishop, since at that time only the bishop presided at the Eucharist. Priests (presbyters) were simply his council of advisors and did not normally preside at the Eucharist. However, as dioceses grew larger and multiple celebrations of the Eucharist were needed, the priests (presbyters) were sent to nearby assemblies to substitute for the bishop. As that became more common, the priest (presbyter) began to be seen as the normal presider at the Eucharist and so came to be called a priest rather than a presbyter.

While that was undoubtedly a valid development, we might note here that it entailed a radical shift in perspective. The terms "presbyter" (meaning "elder") and "bishop" (meaning "overseer") contain a clear reference to the role of those ministries in leading the community in its daily life. While that included leadership in worship, it also involved a much broader ministry. The term "priest," in contrast, seems to define the office solely in terms of worship. Thus, instead of understanding the cultic role as a result of being the community's leader, people began to see the priest more and more as primarily a cultic figure, ordained for sacramental ministry and doing other things in the community only secondarily.

That narrow sacramental focus led to further shifts in understanding orders of ministry in succeeding centuries. Since the priest (presbyter) was increasingly seen as ordained precisely for sacramental ministry, ordination came to be seen more and more as the conferral of the power to consecrate the Eucharist and absolve sins. Some scholars maintain that this was quite a change from the early tradition. Although the historical evidence is not completely clear, they are inclined to believe that deacons and perhaps even laymen could preside at the Eucharist in emergencies and that lay persons could hear confessions in emergencies and anoint the sick with holy oil even in ordinary circumstances. Such historical data seem incredible to us, but the early Church consistently saw the celebration of the sacraments as the work of the whole community, and whoever led the community could preside at those liturgical celebrations. Scholars maintain that such leaders were normally ordained, but in emergencies even a non-ordained leader could preside.

Loss of the community connection

As ordination came to be seen as the conferral of powers, it also came to be seen more and more as an individual matter—a conferral of powers upon an individual regardless of his connection to a particular community of faith. By the time of the Third Lateran Council in 1179 and the Fourth Lateran Council in 1215, the shift was complete. In contrast to the Council of Chalcedon, the Third Lateran Council reduced the community base of ordination to simply a question of whether the one ordained had a bishop who would provide a proper living for him. Thus ordination without a community ministry was approved in practice, if not in theory. The Fourth Lateran Council completed the picture by insisting that no one could preside at the Eucharist except a priest (presbyter) or bishop who had been validly ordained.

Paralleling that narrowing focus of the meaning of ordination was a narrowing of the concept of ministry in the Church. While the early Church had a multiplicity of ministries, ordained and non-ordained, to meet the varied needs of the community, the late medieval Church knew only the ministries of priest (presbyter) and bishop. Deacons, who had once been much more powerful and influential than the priests (presbyters), had disappeared except as a step on the way to priesthood. So, too, the orders of porter, lector, exorcist, acolyte, and subdeacon were transformed from separate orders with their own ministries to being simply steps to the priesthood. Thus the sacrament of holy orders came to be seen as containing seven steps: four minor orders (porter, lector, exorcist, and acolyte) and three major orders (subdeacon, deacon, and priest). In that perspective the office of bishop was seen as simply a consecration of a priest to higher office, though there was considerable discussion about whether that office was a true sacramental order as well. That was the state of things until recent times in the Church.

Recent reforms

The Second Vatican Council initiated a reform of the whole life of the Church, so it was inevitable that it would also affect the ministerial structure of the Church. The Council ordered that both the ceremonies and the texts of the ordination rites be revised, noting specifically that all the bishops present may impose hands at the consecration of a bishop. It also approved the restoration of the diaconate as a permanent order in the Church.

In his apostolic letters *Ministeria quaedam* and *Ad pascendum,* issued on August 15, 1972, Pope Paul VI reformed the structure of ministry in the Church. He suppressed the minor orders, retaining the offices of reader and acolyte as "ministries" rather than orders. A candidate is now "instituted" as a reader or acolyte, not ordained. He also re-established the diaconate as an independent order, open to both single and married men. The old rite of tonsure was replaced by a rite of admission to candidacy for ordination as deacons and priests. The sacrament of holy orders is thus seen as being comprised of the three ancient orders of deacon, priest (presbyter), and bishop.

For many who had been ordained to the old minor orders, it came as a bit of a shock that those orders could simply be suppressed by decree. But that was just another example of the Church reshaping its ministerial structure to meet the changed needs of new situations. The Church has done that regularly throughout history, and perhaps the most important lesson we can draw from this historical overview is that the Church can and must continue to shape its ministries according to the needs of the Church community in every age.

A Return to Our Roots

The period since the Second Vatican Council has seen some gradual trends that are really a return to our roots. One is a growing awareness of the community base of ordained ministry. More and more, bishops, priests (presbyters), and deacons are seeing their office as deeply bound to the people they are called to serve. Priests (presbyters) and bishops are still usually called to ministry without much question of their leadership role in the community from which they come, and they are often assigned to local communities where they are complete strangers when they arrive. The selection of deacon candidates today, however, is usually based on the recognition of their leadership role in the communities from which they come and in which they will continue to serve after ordination. It is possible that a similar process will develop in the future for priests (presbyters) and bishops.

The other trend is a reversal of the concentration of all ministries into the ministry of the priest (presbyter). The restoration of the diaconate and a virtual explosion of lay ministries, both liturgical and pastoral, have given us a much richer and more varied complement of ministerial roles in the Church. Just a few decades ago the pastor performed almost all ministry in the parish; he had all the answers and all the authority. Today many parishes have several people on the staff as well as a host of volunteers, all helping to make decisions about the life of the parish and to carry on the work of the Church in their area.

That expansion of ministries puts the decline in the number of priests (presbyters) in a different light. It may well be that we do not have a real shortage of priests (presbyters) as much as we have the beginnings of a realignment of ministries that can be seen only faintly at this point. It is clear that the Church, in this country at least, has made use of the large number of priests (presbyters) in ways that could well be termed "misuse." They have functioned as teachers of math and science and literature in high schools, as bookkeepers and secretaries and maintenance men in parishes, and as clerks or businessmen in diocesan offices. It might well be argued that many priests (presbyters) have spent a major part of their working life doing tasks for which they were not trained and for which they did not need to be ordained. The ordained priest (presbyter) or bishop is necessary for presiding at the Eucharist and the sacraments of penance and anointing the sick; no one can substitute for him in these roles, and there are many other ministries that are linked to these indispensable sacramental functions, such as visiting the sick, spiritual counseling, and fostering the community's growth in faith. But the ordained clergy also do many tasks that are not related to their training or their orders. The first step, then, in dealing with the "shortage" of clergy is to free them from tasks and ministries that can be properly done by others.

The Meaning of Holy Orders

The other side of that coin, however, helps us to focus the contemporary problematic about the sacrament of holy orders. It arises as a question in the mind of many of the ordained and those who consider entering the ordained ministry: "Why should I be ordained when everybody else can do almost the same things I can do?" In other words, what is the meaning of ordination? Our tradition reveals several principles for answering that question.

First, the question should be phrased, not in terms of what an ordained person can do, but in terms of what place that order of ministry has in the community of faith. Whatever powers are connected with an order flow from the role of that order in the community. Second, it is clear that ordination is the affirmation of a leadership role in the community. Leadership can be exercised in various ways, but an order exists in the Church to provide leadership and guidance for the community. Third, ordination is initiation into an order of peers who are dedicated to serving the community. In that sense holy orders is like Christian marriage. Among the seven sacraments, these two are initiations into states of life within the Church. Thus one does not "receive" the order of bishop or priest (presbyter) or deacon; one "enters" the order.

The Church community celebrates the initiation of one or several of its members into a ministerial order in the liturgical rites of ordination, recognizing the call of the minister as a gift of God and praying for the grace of the Spirit upon those called to serve the community in that sacramental order. In the process of celebrating the call of those individuals, the whole community also reaffirms its own commitment to minister in the name of Christ.

Seeing ordained ministers as sacramental symbols throughout their lives can help us understand what we mean when we speak of their leadership function. While the ordained minister may in fact lead the community in a variety of ways, an order itself functions precisely as sacrament. Sacraments function by signifying, by being symbols. Ordained ministers lead the Church by being living symbols in the midst of the Church community. The orders of ministry are symbols of the wider ministry of the whole Church; their very presence among us reminds us of the responsibility of the whole community to carry on the ministry of Christ in the world today.

The orders of ministry, therefore, exist within the Church primarily for the service of the Church community. It is crucial to recognize that the ordained ministries do not exhaust the ministry of the Church. The whole Church is to minister to the world. Christians do not exist for themselves but to serve all people in Christ's name. The responsibility for ministry flows from their very membership in the Church. The orders of ministry exist within the Church to support the rest of the community in carrying out the wider ministry of the Church. For too long we have tended to see all ministry as belonging to the ordained, but the orders exist as symbols of the much larger ministry of the whole Church.

Deacon, Priest (Presbyter), and Bishop

The next logical question is, What aspect of that ministry is symbolized by each order? What is the difference between deacons, priests (presbyters), and bishops? Looking again at the ordination rites themselves gives us a few clues. Deacons are ordained, as their name suggests (*diakonein* = "to serve"), to focus the community's ministry of service or charity. "As deacons," the bishop tells them, "you will serve Jesus Christ, who was known among his disciples as the one who served others. Do the will of God generously. Serve God and mankind in love and joy. . . . Like the men the apostles chose for works of charity, you should be men of good reputation, filled with wisdom and the Holy Spirit." Deacons are not the only ones in the community who carry out charitable activities, but their ministry to the poor, the sick, the grieving, the imprisoned, and the oppressed stands as a constant witness to all of us that this is an essential part of Christ's mission and thus of the Church's work.

Bishops are ordained, again as their name suggests (*episkopos* = "overseer"), to guide the work of the Church, to govern the community and to coordinate the various ministries of the body. "As a steward of the mysteries of Christ in the church," the new bishop is told, "be a faithful overseer and guardian. Since you are chosen by the Father to rule over his family, always be mindful of the Good Shepherd, who knows his sheep and is known by them and who did not hesitate to lay down his life for them. . . . Encourage the faithful to work with you in your apostolic task; listen willingly to what they have to say. . . . Never forget that in the Catholic Church . . .

you are incorporated into the college of bishops. You should therefore have a constant concern for all the churches and gladly come to the aid and support of churches in need. Attend to the whole flock in which the Holy Spirit appoints you an overseer of the Church of God. . . ." The last point underscores the bishop's role in maintaining the link between the local churches and having a concern for the universal Church.

When it comes to the order of priest (presbyter), the name is less helpful. "Presbyter" means "elder," but that does not indicate his role very clearly. The rites of ordination, too, are less clear about the unique role of the priest (presbyter), stressing his role as co-worker with the bishop. "He is called to share in the priesthood of the bishops and to be molded into the likeness of Christ. . . . As a co-worker with the order of bishops may he be faithful to the ministry that he receives from you, Lord God, and be to others a model of right conduct. May he be faithful in working with the order of bishops, so that the words of the Gospel may reach the ends of the earth. . . ." What we find here is in accord with the history of the presbyterate. Priests (presbyters) performed the functions of the bishop in other communities when the bishop could not be present to all the assemblies under his care. The order of priest (presbyter), then, seems to symbolize the same aspects of ministry as that of bishop, but in a local community rather than the whole diocese. The priest (presbyter) is a "sub-bishop," one might say. The role of the pastor in a parish seems to revolve around three areas: preaching the Word of God, presiding at Mass and the sacraments, and fostering the growth of the Christian community; those are also the tasks of the bishop for the whole diocese.

Principles for the Future

When we become aware of the changes that have occurred in the shape of ministries in our history, it becomes apparent that new orders can be developed. We have had five other orders in the past, not to mention the variety of ministries listed in the New Testament. The Church has the power, and indeed the obligation, to institute whatever orders are necessary for carrying on the ministry of Christ in every age.

At this point it may be possible to suggest some principles for the continuing development of Church ministry in the future. The first, which we have not mentioned explicitly yet, is the centrality of the Eucharist for the life of the Christian community. Our very existence as a Church revolves around the Sunday Eucharist. We believe that this is not optional but essential to being the Church that Christ intends us to be. A corollary of that principle is that every local Church community has the right to the regular celebration of the Eucharist. As many commentators have noted, that right is much more basic than any optional criteria for who may be ordained. It is clear, for example, from our history and from the continuous practice of the Eastern Rites, that celibacy is not essential for ordination to the presbyterate. To continue to insist on such criteria while depriving many local churches of the right to weekly Eucharist seems hard to justify theologically or pastorally.

Our tradition teaches us that the Church can ordain married men or celibates; it can ordain clergy to function full-time or part-time while they are engaged in other occupations. The Holy See does not think it is possible to ordain women, but other Christian Churches and many Roman Catholic theologians disagree with that position. The discussion of that issue will undoubtedly continue in the years ahead, and the outcome of the debate is not clear. In any case, all those who are ordained ought to be truly leaders of Church communities. No individuals should be ordained for their own sake, no matter how clearly they feel called. All those ordained should be ordained to the service of Church communities and ought to be closely bound to those communities. That does not imply that one can serve only the parish or even the diocese from which one comes. The Church has always recognized that the good of the greater Church could justify a transfer to another community. But that was by way of exception rather than the general rule.

Another way to look at this is to suggest that those who are the community's leaders ought to be ordained. If a community develops its own leadership, which faithfully ministers to the Church, perhaps those very leaders, after some training and examination of their lives, should be affirmed and ratified by the liturgical rites of ordination.

A final principle we might enunciate is that those initiated into the various orders need real bonds of shared ministry with others in that same order. Those who share the same order of ministry need to share prayer with one another, socialize together, and support one another in their work. That need is becoming evident among priests (presbyters) today as more and more of them function in one-man parishes and easily become isolated from the rest of their order. In some cases that may mean developing shared living arrangements; other times it will mean special gatherings and efforts to maintain communication and contact. However it is fostered, the orders of ministry must be real groups of peers supporting one another in their life and work and prayer.

One Possible Model

I would like to conclude this chapter with a possible model of ordained ministry in our country in the years ahead. This is not so much a prophecy as a hint of the kinds of changes the Lord may have in store for us. The model I propose is suggested by current trends, but it is not a sure bet. The actual shape of ministry can only be worked out in practice by the living Church under the guidance of the Holy Spirit. The value of such a model is simply to open us up to a wider range of possibilities so that we will be open to the Spirit's leading.

As the number of priests (presbyters) declines, more and more of them are being asked to take responsibility for two or more parishes, and this trend will clearly increase in the years ahead. Many pastors are concerned about that, fearing that they will become simply "sacrament machines," running from parish to parish with little real contact with the daily life of the people. That would produce both bad liturgy and poor ministry. If we begin to imagine, however, a full-time, professional minister with responsibility for five or ten parishes, we can recognize that role as the function of the bishop in the early centuries of the Church. Perhaps what we now know as full-time, intensively trained, professional clergy will in the future be ordained bishops, with responsibility for mini-dioceses of five or ten parishes. In that case, our current bishops would become metropolitans, or heads of episcopal provinces.

If we couple that shift with the trend toward smaller and more intimate parish communities (some would suggest six hundred families as a maximum for any real sense of community), then it becomes obvious that we will need to ordain others as priests (presbyters) to provide for the daily leadership of the local parishes. Those leaders might well be either full-time or part-time, married or celibate, (men or women?) and might best be chosen from the natural leadership of the community. With some training (perhaps like that now given to permanent deacons) and continual guidance from the local bishop, they would also, of course, preside at the Eucharist and the regular celebration of the other sacraments. (The ministry of confessor, requiring special personality and skills, might well become a separate ministry.) The local bishop, having only five or ten parishes in his diocese, would be actively involved in the life of those parishes, providing theological expertise, training and coordinating the various ministries (including the priest-presbyters), stimulating the spiritual growth of the Church, and taking special care to see that each local church stays in close contact with neighboring churches and with the universal Church.

Among other things, this model would enable bishops to fulfill the beautiful vision of their role spelled out in the Second Vatican Council and in the revised liturgical rites. So often now those ideals remain mere theory because dioceses are much too large for the bishop to be the actual father of the local Church, presiding over the rites of initiation, gathering the whole local Church together for special celebrations, etc. Few Catholics even see their bishop once a year, which is woefully inadequate for the role the Church has described for the bishop.

In addition to the provincial bishops, local bishops, and parish priests (presbyters), this model also assumes the ministry of a whole variety of other members of the Church. Some would be ordained (e.g., deacons), others non-ordained. Some would be full-time and paid, others would be part-time and voluntary. One cannot begin to describe or limit them in advance, for they would likely vary from one parish to the next as each Church community works out the best ways to meet the needs of its own area. In general, however, we might suggest that they would look something like the ministers in the New Testament, including evangelizers, teachers, administrators, caretakers, ministers to the sick, confessors, worship planners, prayer leaders, bereavement ministers, youth ministers, ushers, musicians, sacristans, prison visitors, ministers to the poor, etc.

To some, such a model may sound radical and frightening. To others, though, it offers hope for the future growth and vitality of the Church. Change is never easy, but it is of the essence of ministry to change to meet the changing needs of the Church. Such an attitude of selfless service is a fundamental prerequisite for good ministry, whatever shape it takes. May the Spirit of God fill us all with the will to serve God and one another in humility and with the willingness to die to self that Christ himself manifested, for he came not to be served but to serve, and to give his life for the salvation of all.

DISCUSSION/REFLECTION QUESTIONS

1. Do you see the declining number of priests in our country as a crisis or an opportunity? Do we really have a "priest shortage"?

2. Why was the community connection to ordination so important in the early Church? Do you think we need to recover a stronger community base for ministry? How can it be done?

3. What advantages and disadvantages can you see if all deacons and priests came back to serve the parish from which they were called to ordination?

4. How many different ministries are functioning in your parish today? Can you remember when all those ministries were the work of the priest? Which way do you think is better? Why?

5. What does it mean for a person to be ordained? How would you explain ordination to a young student?

6. Can you explain the differences between the orders of deacon, presbyter, and bishop?

7. How important is the weekly Eucharist in the life of your parish? In your own spiritual life? Do you think the Church should ordain women or married men rather than have parishes without weekly Sunday Eucharist?

8. What do you think the Church's ministerial structure will be like in the year 2000? Does the model presented in this chapter make sense to you?

9. How do you share in the ministry of the Church? Can you foresee other ways in which you could be involved in the ongoing work of Christ?

10. Are the ordained ministers you know helpful to you in carrying out your own Christian ministry? How could they be more helpful? How can you help them in their ministry?